The SOUL of the Story

The Soul of the Story

the Story

Meetings with Remarkable People

Rabbi David Zeller

For People of All Faiths, All Backgrounds

JEWISH LIGHTS Publishing

Woodstock, Vermont

www.jewishlights.com

The Soul of the Story:
Meetings with Remarkable People

2006 First Printing
© 2006 by David Zeller

Library of Congress Cataloging-in-Publication Data

Zeller, David, 1946–
The soul of the story : meetings with remarkable people / by David Zeller.
p. cm.
Includes bibliographical references and index.
ISBN 1-58023-272-8 (alk. paper)
1. Zeller, David, 1946—Travel. 2. Spiritual biography. 3. Zeller, David, 1946—Relations with religious leaders. 4. Religious leaders. 5. East and West. 6. Spiritual life—Judaism. 7. Psychology and religion. I. Title.
BM755.Z385.A3 2005
296.8'32092—dc22

2005027388

10   9   8   7   6   5   4   3   2   1
Manufactured in the United States of America
Jacket Design: Jenny Buono

For People of All Faiths, All Backgrounds
Published by Jewish Lights Publishing
A Division of LongHill Partners, Inc.
Sunset Farm Offices, Route 4, P.O. Box 237
Woodstock, VT 05091
Tel: (802) 457-4000   Fax: (802) 457-4004
www.jewishlights.com

"The world says: Stories are meant to help you sleep. But I say: Stories are meant to wake you up!"

—Rebbe Nachman of Breslov

"God created the world ... with story."

—*Sefer Yetzirah*

"The power of a story reaches beyond our minds, penetrates even deeper than our hearts. It *mamash* [really] touches our souls.... Because in the end, the most important knowledge is not scientific, or even mystical; it's to know what life is all about. And that's the essence of a story—understanding life."

—Reb Shlomo Carlebach

DEDICATION

These stories are dedicated to the memory of my grandparents, murdered in the Holocaust, who could never tell me their stories; to my father, Max Mordechai Zeller, *z"l*, who kindled the lights of the Hanukkah menorah and of my psyche with such dedication; and to my rebbe, Shlomo Carlebach, *zt"l*, for kindling the light of my Jewish *neshama* and telling us all the stories of our people, rebbes, and souls.

These stories are dedicated to my mother, Lore Zeller, for the neverending story of her love, care, and generosity; may the story of your life keep unfolding for many years to come.

These stories are dedicated with deep gratitude and love to my wife, Hannah-Sara; thank you for your steady support through all the ups and downs of this intensive time of writing.

CONTENTS

INTRODUCTION

FIRE ON THE MOUNTAIN:
The Wanderer

■ I Had Become a Hasidic Story

A few years ago, I had a wonderful Shabbat dinner with members of a Hasidic community in Brooklyn. Since many of us did not know each other, we were asked to introduce ourselves. In telling about myself, I mentioned that after living for two years in Israel and then a year in India, I'd returned to the West, ready to integrate the worlds of East and West, psychology and religion, the intellectual and the meditative, the inner and the outer, and, especially, Judaism and spirituality. "Oh!" my host said. "You've got to hear the story of the Jew who met the Shinto priest!" He began to tell the story, when I interrupted, asking whether he would like *me* to tell the story. When he asked why, I explained that the story was about *me*, and that I was the one who had originally told it years ago.

I had become a Hasidic story. This was a sign that it was time for me to tell my own stories, stories of my meetings with remarkable souls, stories of how they had remarkably affected my own soul. That, in fact, is what I am doing now. That is why I am telling this to you now.

■ An Orthodox Jungian and a Reform Jew

I was raised an orthodox Jungian and a Reform Jew. Through a lot of wandering and wondering, I became an Orthodox Jew and a reform Jungian.

Reform Jew because, though my family had a very strong sense of Jewish identity—my father was briefly held in a concentration camp and later my parents escaped the Holocaust—other than Hanukkah and a Passover seder, we observed few Jewish traditions while growing up. I hadn't even heard of the Sabbath or of dietary laws, and I had no real awareness of Israel. We had joined a Reform temple only so I could have a bar mitzvah. But there was very little learning about Judaism in my family. Like any bar mitzvah boy, I learned to chant a small part of my Torah portion. It had little meaning for me, and it was the last time I was in a synagogue for many years.

Orthodox Jungian because my father and almost all our family friends were therapists who followed the theories of C.G. Jung, the psychiatrist who had broken with Freud and started his own depth psychology, a broader, deeper approach to the human psyche, the Self, and the Soul. Jungians work very intimately with various aspects of the unconscious, inner and often hidden dimensions of the Self or Soul, from beyond the limitations of our more superficial physical and ego-identity world. I was raised and nurtured amid dream interpretation, astrology, cheirology (palm reading), graphology (handwriting analysis), fairy tales, and myths. All this contributed to the magic of my childhood. It wasn't until I was older that I discovered my parents were really "nuts" and that most kids' parents didn't do those kinds of things!

■ *I Ching*: The Wanderer

When I was around fifteen, my father asked what I wanted to do after finishing high school. I told him I didn't know, though everyone seemed to go to college automatically, without giving it too much thought. It appeared that *he* had given it quite a bit of thought and suggested that we ask the *I Ching* (pronounced "ee-ching"). "What's the *I Ching*?" I asked. He explained that it was an ancient Chinese book of wisdom that is used for divination or clarifying the future. He explained that you focus on your question and then toss three coins, six times. According to the combination of heads and tails that ensues, you get two sets of three lines each, either solid or broken. Then you look up that combination of lines in the *I Ching* to see what it predicts. Having already been exposed to astrology, cheirology, graphology and dream interpretation, I shouldn't have been surprised that there were still more ways to understand our character and our lives. But I was.

I threw the coins. It came out—"Fire on the Mountain: the Wanderer." My father quickly interpreted this to mean that I would wander through the heights and depths of academia. Obviously, he had given this question a *lot* of thought. My father was a great therapist to his clients, but thank God, around his children, he could still be just an irrational parent.

Well, I did go to college. And I did a bit of wandering while I was there. I started in pre-med and psychology, as all our Jungian friends and, of course, my father had recommended: "Become a good psychiatrist in order to make the best contribution to the world of Jungian psychology." It was the tough pre-med requirements that drove me to take physics in summer school at the University of California, Berkeley, in 1966. That brought me to the Berkeley Folk Festival, which led to my life-changing meeting with Rabbi Shlomo Carlebach. Shlomo was an Orthodox rabbi from New York, who composed original, uplifting, and deeply inspiring melodies from Jewish liturgy. He told stories and gave teachings that touched and opened the hearts of so many searching young adults like myself. I had a spiritual and transformative experience dancing and singing with him; as a result, I dropped the pre-med and switched to psychology and religion. The "pre-medical" was on the way to becoming "pre-meditation."

Looking back now, I can see that all this was a process of wandering and wondering, and wandering and wondering some more. From the theoretical world of Jungian maps of consciousness, I had danced into the more experiential world of consciousness and spirituality. Following those first spiritual experiences with Shlomo, I sought more experiences from other teachers and other practices. This led to two years in Israel doing organizational development and human relations work for the kibbutz movement. Then I spent a year in India where I became a sadhu, living outside in nature and bathing in the rivers. A sadhu is like a monk who lives totally in the hands of God. For me, it was the final letting go of the "me" that I was still identifying with from my Western upbringing. From American campus to Israeli kibbutz was one thing, but from Western materialism to Eastern spirituality was something entirely different. I was shocked by how easily I made the transformation, and how much I felt "at home." Nonetheless, profound Jewish experiences I had in India determined my final orientation toward my true home in Judaism.

In the summer of 1972 I returned to the U.S. to turn seemingly opposing worlds into complementary worlds: integrating East and West, psychology and spirituality, the theoretical and the experiential. And I was determined to integrate Judaism with all of them. From 1972 to 1981, as a pioneer in transpersonal psychology, I helped establish the first accredited BA and PhD programs in transpersonal psychology at Johnston College in Redlands, California, and then at the Institute of Transpersonal Psychology in Palo Alto, California. I brought Jewish mystical teachings and practices into transpersonal psychology, which until then had mainly been built on Buddhist, Yogic, and Sufi spiritual maps and teachings; and I brought transpersonal psychology back into the world of Judaism, which had lost much of its own psychological and spiritual foundations. In 1981 I founded the Network of Conscious Judaism, and in 1985, I moved to Israel to continue my East/West/Jewish integration there.

My father and I had no idea just how much I would wander geographically, academically, and spiritually. I still had much to learn and understand about that image from the prediction in the *I Ching*. I had wandered from the ordinary, to the psychological, to the spiritual.

■ My Changing Portion: From Spying to Singing

Yet, there was a system of divination, of future tuning, that I had encountered even before the *I Ching*, but that I wasn't really aware of until years later: the selection of my Torah portion for my bar mitzvah! Nearly twenty years later, I was with Reb Zalman Schachter (later he changed his name to Schachter-Shalomi). He liked to call people up to the Torah who had an important question about their lives. He would ask them to roll the Torah back and forth, open it, and see what was written. *That* was the answer to their question.

Your true Torah parasha comes from the portion of the Torah that is read on the Shabbat following your birth. But sometimes circumstances arise and the date for the bar or bat mitzvah is changed to a different parasha than that of your birth. In my case, because of the year I spent with my parents in Switzerland when I was eleven, my bar mitzvah was delayed half a year to allow the necessary time for me to attend Hebrew and Judaism classes. So I was given a different date that could affect my fate.

My birth parasha is *Shlach L'cha* ("Send for Yourself"). It tells of the *m'rag'lim*, the spies, whom Moses had sent to check out the Promised Land and report back to the people who were waiting in the desert. The spies' negative report frightened the people. The lack of higher vision on the part of the spies, and the lack of faith in God and Moses on the part of the Hebrew people, created the weakness, the chink in the armor through which the Holy Temple would be destroyed in the future. We commemorate that day, known as Tisha b'Av, the ninth of Av, with a day of fasting. That is my birth Torah portion. And there are infinite positive aspects and spins to that parasha as well.

My new parasha, *B'Shalach* ("When they were sent"), dealt with the splitting of the Red Sea, with Moses and the people of

Israel singing a song of praise, "the Song of the Sea," to God after crossing over and reaching safety. That Shabbat is called *Shabbat Shira*, the Sabbath of Song. My "portion" switched from misperception and calamity to breakthrough and song.

At the time, I didn't understand what the words meant in Hebrew, so this really didn't mean anything special to me. I knew so little about Judaism or Torah or what a bar mitzvah meant in terms of entering a committed relationship with God and the Torah and its mitzvot (commandments). Most people understand *mitzvah* to come from the word *tzav* (command). Today, I understand *mitzvah* as coming from *tzavtah* (to join), meaning actions that fuse or join the individual to the Divine. Perhaps it's the illusion of our separateness and alienation from, or disbelief in, the Divine that makes us feel so confused, un-fused, dis-jointed, or dis-joined.

While singing my parasha for my bar mitzvah, I discovered that I had a good voice. Within a few years, I was singing in my high school choir and taking voice lessons. I continued to sing throughout college, in choir, in glee club, in a barbershop quartet, and in a folk jug-band called "The Mable Shaw Bridges Memorial Skiffle Society." Singing was the greatest gift I got from God for my bar mitzvah.

■ The Song of the Sea

Song is an essential part of Judaism—from the Song of the Sea to the songs that accompanied all the services in the Holy Temple in Jerusalem. *Psukei d'zimra* (the verses of song) is the largest part of morning prayers and comes right before the section of prayer that contains the *Sh'ma*, the declaration of God's Oneness. And although you can just read the Torah on Shabbat, it is meant to be sung to a special melody. According to kabbalistic teachings from the "Four Worlds," melody pours forth from the highest of levels. The first level is the "Letter," which is like our body; second, the "Crown" embellishing the letter corresponds to our emotions. Third, the "Vowels" under the letter parallel our breath of life. Finally, the "Melody" of the letter or word represents our soul.

The *Sea* is one of the great symbols for Torah, suggesting its vast breadth and depth. And my parasha told of the splitting of the Red Sea, a metaphor for penetrating to the deepest, most mystical levels of understanding the Torah.

So my Torah parasha, long before my *I Ching* "parasha," foretold of my Song of the Sea. Not just my unique way of singing from my soul, but also of my symbolically reaching a melodious and mystical interpretation of the Sea, of the Torah, and of learning how to *see* people and events around me in a deeper and more spiritual way.

Only at this writing did I realize that I went from *Shlach L'cha*, "*to send* someone in your stead," to *B'Shalach*, "*being sent* yourself." Both are about "sending." One was sending people to check it out *for* you, instead of seeing it for yourself or simply having faith in God, "sight unseen." The other, *B'Shalach*, was when Pharaoh—the controller, the ego—releases you from *his* control into true freedom: to see it for *yourself.* Then, you are on your spiritual journey to the Holy Mountain; then, you are ready to experience the Fire on the Mountain. We go from being a slave to Pharaoh to being a servant of God. From a birth parasha of being frightened about Israel, I've come to love it and live in it. And instead of crying over it, I'm singing in it and singing my praises of it.

■ Fire on the Mountain

Years after that first reading with my father, I took another look at the symbol in the *I Ching*—"Fire on the Mountain: the Wanderer." *Fire on the Mountain!* Could there be a stronger symbol for Judaism and for the Jewish people? *Fire on the Mountain*—a symbol of the fire upon which Abraham sacrificed the ram that replaced Isaac, whom Abraham had been ready to offer up at God's command. *Fire on the Mountain*—for Moses and the burning bush! *Fire on the Mountain*—for the lightning and thunder at Sinai at the time of the revelation of all revelations!

And *"the Wanderer!"* We Jewish people have been called "the wandering people" for centuries: for Abraham's journey from Ur Chasdim to the Land of Israel; for our shepherding ancestors who wandered the land grazing their sheep; for wandering forty years in the wilderness from Egyptian slavery back to the Promised Land; and for our wandering in exile in the Diaspora for two thousand years after the destruction of the Holy Temple in Jerusalem. Also, I might add, we could be called "the *wondering* people," and the "One-dering" people, seeing the Oneness of God in all of creation.

Additionally, we are called the "Hebrew people," *Ivrim.* "Hebrew" comes from the word *iver* (pronounced "ee-ver"), meaning "to cross over." *Iver* is very likely the ancient linguistic root of the English word *over.* We aren't wandering aimlessly. We have direction and purpose. We are crossing *over,* overcoming the illusion of duality (of the Tree of Knowledge of opposites) and returning to the unity and oneness (of the Tree of Life). We are reaching beyond the outer material world, bridging that with the inner spiritual world, bridging ancient and modern cultures and traditions. It has taken years for me to appreciate my Torah parasha and my *I Ching* hexagram. Now I savor them from a uniquely Jewish perspective, one that daily sustains and enriches me.

These images from the *I Ching* and the Song of the Sea reached far beyond anything I could have imagined or dreamed of. They seemed to foretell so much of the essence of my life, intuiting and anticipating the many routes and passages and doorways I would cross over and through, and the many extraordinary people and events I would encounter, embrace, and enjoy along the way.

This book is a collection of some of the stories of my life. Most are encounters with remarkable people and nature. A few are more biographical, bridging gaps in the flow of the stories.

Stories are called "stories" because they *store* information, images, memories, dreams, and experiences from the past and even from the future. Stories store something for everyone. May my stories stir what's stored in *your* soul. May they help you wake up to the wonders of *your own* life's experiences. May you tell my stories to others. May you tell *your* stories to others. May you, too, become a Hasidic story!

1

MY MOTHER AND FATHER:
Growing Up with Dreams

We're about to meet some pretty remarkable souls, people who taught me, challenged me, fascinated me; they made me, in one way or another, who I am today. But it is not an exaggeration to say that I wouldn't have met them—or could not have been open enough to them—if it wasn't for the first two most remarkable souls in my life: my mother and my father.

My father always took the time to listen to my dreams. Whether in the middle of the night or early in the morning, or, really, any time of day, he was ready to listen. I took this for granted, not knowing how rare it was for parents to make room for their children's dreams. That is as true about the dreams we have when we sleep as well as the dreams and fantasies and hopes we have when we are awake. Often, children are told, "Go back to bed. It's the middle of the night!" Or, "It's only a dream. Don't pay any attention to it." Or, "Stop daydreaming. Wake up to reality!"

At first, my dad would just listen. As I got older, he would offer a simple interpretation. Older still, he'd first ask me what I thought it meant, then add his own understanding.

I often saw my father sitting at home, working on his clients' dreams or the drawings they may have made depicting images from their dreams. A Jungian psychologist, he did therapy with people throughout the week. These weren't necessarily the drawings of accomplished artists; they were the expression of the Self or Soul.

Dad's interest in dreams went back quite a way. He became a lawyer in Germany in 1929, but he was thrown out of the Berlin courts three years later by the Nazi regime because he was a Jew. His work with people stimulated his interest in the dynamics of the human personality. He began his own therapy, but dissatisfied with how his therapist dealt with dreams, he left to work with an early student of Jung's and began studying depth psychology. He also studied graphology, understanding personality by analyzing handwriting.

He worked in his father's fabric company while pursuing these studies. In fact, he met my mother through her handwritten application for a secretarial job there. He was so struck by the personality that shined through her handwriting that they interviewed her and she got the job. They married in 1936 in Berlin, and my father completed his training as a Jungian analyst two years later.

On *Kristallnacht*, the night of the shattered glass of Jewish shop windows throughout Germany in November 1938, he was called to the local police station on false pretenses, and then sent to Sacksenhausen, the concentration camp just outside Berlin.

Not long after he arrived, he had a dream: Hitler came to him and shook his hand. With his knowledge of Jungian dream interpretation—despite the frightening and unknown situation he was in—he interpreted the dream to mean that Hitler would not defeat him, that somehow he would survive this ordeal.

Dad had a few things working in his favor, though he didn't know it at the time. Within days after he was taken, my mother, who was now alone with my older brother (who was less than one year old at the time), told a taxi driver to drive around the perimeter of the concentration camp. He followed her instructions, but at some point stopped and asked her, "Why are you doing this? This is very risky."

"My husband was just taken by the Gestapo," she answered. "I assume he's here, and I was hoping he'd be outside by the fence. I just want to let him know that our baby and I are alright. I don't want him to worry about us!"

"Young woman, you want my advice? It is very dangerous for you—and maybe even for me—to be driving around here. Why don't you send him a postcard, and tell him you're okay? You know, we Germans are so efficient that it wouldn't surprise me if they actually deliver the card to him! Worst comes to worse, you've lost three cents on a postcard."

She sent the postcard. And sure enough, they delivered it! And he was reassured that they were safe.

More than that, his twenty-two-year-old wife, my mother, was already on a brave mission of her own to have him released. She went to a travel agent and asked to buy one-way tickets for herself, her husband, and their baby boy.

The agent asked, "Can I see your visas please?"

"We don't have our visa yet," she answered.

"Can I see your visa waiting number, please?"

She showed her their number on the waiting list to receive visas.

"But, these numbers won't come up for a very long time. Your tickets will have expired by then."

"Let me worry about that. The SS wants to see that we are making efforts to leave. All you have to do is sell me the tickets."

Tickets in hand, she went to Gestapo headquarters in Berlin and requested that her husband be released from the concentration camp, as the family was making plans to leave the country.

The officer in charge said, "Show me your tickets."

She showed him the tickets.

"Show me your visas."

"We don't have our visa yet."

"Show me your visa waiting number."

She showed him the number.

"But, these numbers won't come up for a very long time. Your tickets won't be good by then."

She began crying. "You want proof that we are trying to leave the country. Well, *here's* the proof."

"Go away! Come back tomorrow," he said curtly, dismissing her.

She returned the next day, and the secretary handed her a letter that essentially said, "Please release Max Zeller, as his family is completing the necessary steps to leave the country." She looked at the letter in disbelief. Had the SS officer made an error? Had he processed too many people yesterday and lost track of the details? Or was he possibly being compassionate toward a young woman who was a wife and a mother? One thing was certain: She would not ask him how this could be! She went home and waited.

A few weeks later, my father was released. He had to report to the Gestapo regularly, and if he wasn't out of the country in six months, they would send him back to the concentration camp.

More miracles resulted from a letter my mother sent to a distant relative in London, who had accidentally bumped into someone on a train in England. He apologized to the stranger. Noting his German accent, the stranger asked, "Are you German?"

"I'm not German," he replied, "I'm *Jewish*, originally from Germany."

"Is it true what's happening to the Jews in Germany? We hear rumors, but it's impossible to know for certain."

Mom's cousin showed him the letter from my mother that described what was going on.

"I head a large bank, and many of my friends are also bankers. We would like to help people by being their legal and financial sponsors so they can get their British visas. But without specific names, there is nothing we can do. Can you give me some names?"

Our cousin sat down and wrote out the names of all his relatives. My parents and my brother were the last ones on his list. And so, totally unrelated to their visa waiting-list number, they received a call from the British Embassy in Berlin, informing them to stop by for their British visas.

Somehow, they survived the blitzkrieg, the almost nonstop German bombing of London, and then, through more miracles, they took the perilous and freezing steamship journey to America in January 1941 during the war, dodging German U-boats. From New York, they bussed across the country to Los Angeles, where they began a whole new life.

Between Dad's *dream* and, more important, Mom's refusal to accept this *nightmare,* they lived to see children and grandchildren, and my mother, thank God, to see great-grandchildren.

Years later, my mother came to visit me and my family after I had moved to Israel. The same day that an ultrasound test confirmed that my wife, Hannah-Sara, was pregnant, my mother, my wife, and I went to Yad VaShem, the Holocaust museum in Jerusalem. There we found records that had recently been released from Berlin, listing the deportation and death of my four grandparents and many of our extended family. We left with heavy hearts. It's not that we hadn't known that they had all been murdered in the Holocaust. But this was the first time we had seen their names in the Nazis' own immaculate records. Walking away from Yad VaShem, my mother turned to my wife and said, simply and quietly, "Thank you for bringing another Zeller into the world."

So, dreams, aspirations, and inspirations meant much to our family. And when my father asked me, "Tell me your dreams," I knew he was there, really listening to me. Because he listened so attentively there are a number of childhood dreams that I can still remember. His attentiveness permanently etched my dreams into my consciousness.

CARL JUNG:
Seeing the Great Man

I grew up in a house with Jung's picture in almost every room, and his books everywhere. Almost all our family friends were Jungian therapists, and my father went every few years to Zurich—the Jungian's Mecca, or should I say Jerusalem—to do intense therapy with his therapist and to have as many sessions with Jung as possible.

In 1949, my father was there for three months. At the end of his stay, he described the following dream and his interaction with Jung:

> A temple of vast dimensions was in the process of being built. As far as I could see—ahead, behind, right, and left—there were incredible numbers of people building on a pillar. The whole building process was in its very first beginnings, but the foundation was already there. The rest of the building was starting to go up, and I and many others were working on it.

> Jung said, "Ja, you know, that is the temple we all build on. We don't know the people because, believe me, they build in India and China and in Russia and all over the world. That is the new religion. You know how long it will take until it is built?"

> "How should I know? Do you know?"

He said, "I know."

"How long will it take?"

"About six hundred years."

"Where do you know this from?"

"From dreams. From other people's dreams and from my own. This new religion will come together as far as we can see."[1]

Six years later, in 1956, our whole family went to live for a year in Switzerland while my father was on sabbatical in Zurich, studying at the Jung Institute and engaged in intense therapy with his therapist and Jung.

This was my opportunity to meet the great man myself. I wrote a very serious ten-year-old kind of letter to Jung, asking to meet him. I got an answer from his secretary that sort of reached out, tousled my hair, called me a cute kid, and said Jung was very busy. I understood that she meant *too* busy.

Then, a breakthrough: the tenth anniversary of the Jung Institute was coming up. *He* would be there, and my mother's analyst was driving him from his home in Küsnacht. She would tell him who I was, and that I was waiting for him in front of the Institute. It was all set. Then the day came and I had a high fever. But somehow I braved the journey by street-car and waited shivering in the rain for Jung's arrival.

His car pulled up, and out bounced this huge man whom I had only known from the neck up, in photographs. Jung was a sprightly eighty-two, with a twinkle in his eyes. Towering over me, he said, "So, *you* must be Max Zeller's son!"

Looking up to him (literally and figuratively), I said, "I've heard so much about you. I've really been looking forward to meeting you."

He smiled, took a step back, opened his arms out wide as if presenting himself, and said, "Well, what do you think?"

I was speechless, which was very rare for me even when I was ten. This was my first "Zen experience." This wasn't following the normal, logical, social formalities my mind was expecting. Jung's unpretentiousness, his humor, and his humanness have remained with me and, indeed, have left a deep impression. And though I can now claim that Jung consulted me, wanting to know what I think, I'm still working on formulating my answer to him.

Jung has followed me most of my life, through my parents. During my hippie rebellion, with my long hair and cool clothes, I was always reminded about Jung at his eightieth birthday party at the Jung Institute: Each time someone new arrived for the party, Jung pulled himself out of his chair and greeted him or her personally.

People constantly said to him, "Professor Jung, you don't have to be so formal and get up each time someone new comes in the room. It's really okay."

And he would answer, "All my life I've tried to be as conventional as possible, because I need my energy for more important things."

"You see," my parents would say to me, whenever they told this story, "it's better to be conventional and free yourself up for the truly creative and revolutionary things in life."

My mother and father later told me that Jung was asked whether he wanted to take psychedelic substances such as LSD to explore the depths of the unconscious "from inside." Declining the offer, he essentially said that he had a deep commitment to shed light on every image or experience that comes from that great collective unconscious, and that he couldn't even keep up with what he gets through his dreams and active imagination on a daily basis, let alone what came to him through his patients. Psychedelics, he implied, would just further overload him.

And when I was in India, my parents sent me quotes of Jung, explaining why, though he had written introductions to many classic Eastern texts, he had never gone to the Far East. He had to travel the inner route of his own Western religion, he said, because that was the language through which his Soul spoke.

Interestingly enough, when I came back from India, the Jungian clubs and institutes in a number of cities were the first venues to invite me to share the stories of my experiences. My dad still lamented a little that his wandering son had wandered away from academia, and that I had not gotten my MA or PhD or MD. So seeing that I was standing at the front of the "class" speaking to Jungians gave him an unexpected satisfaction, even though I had arrived there by a totally different kind of wandering.

"Well, Dad, what do you think?"

3

SHLOMO CARLEBACH: Awakening My Soul

I have to admit that, while majoring in psychology and pre-med as an undergraduate at Pomona College in Southern California, my grades were not great. The truth was that while I was very interested in Jung's psychology of personality, dreams, and symbolism that I had been exposed to in my childhood, Jung barely existed in Pomona's psychology department. My college advisor was into experimental psych. He smoked and drank excessively and constantly bounced his legs in nervous tension. He did tell me that I should be majoring in "screwing up." (His language was more coarse that that.) On the other hand, very little attracted me to studies in pre-med. I was taking it only because my father and his friends *strongly* recommended it if I wanted to make a real contribution in their field.

If I hadn't been in pre-med, I wouldn't have had to face physics. At Pomona, there was only one physics class, and it was for physics majors. The head of the physics department understood that I was weak in science and advised me to go to the University of California, Berkeley, for summer session to take "physics for non-physics majors," better known as "Mickey Mouse physics."

And so in the summer of 1966, I went to Berkeley. It was the right moment to be there. Everything was starting to happen: At Berkeley itself, there was the nascent student rights movement, and across the bay in San Francisco, there was the nascent hippie movement in Haight-Ashbury. Little did I know what awaited me.

Berkeley was also the place of the Berkeley Folk Festival. And I loved American folk music. While my generation was listening to the music of the late 1950s and early 1960s, my brother, Dan (who is nine years older than me), had given me a proper education in real folk music. My parents raised me as an orthodox Jungian; my brother raised me as an orthodox folksinger. I adored Woody Guthrie, Leadbelly, Cisco Houston, Sonny Terry and Brownie McGee, Ramblin' Jack Elliot and Pete Seeger, and Bob Dylan slipped in just under the wire. The Weavers were fine, but the Kingston Trio, the Limelighters, and other groups like that were way too slick and commercial for purists like us.

Student protests, hippie happenings, Mickey Mouse physics—what interested me most was the Berkeley Folk Festival, which was featuring all my folk heroes. I scraped together all my money—which wasn't much—and bought a full ticket so I could attend all the concerts and workshops.

On opening night, a sampler concert featured five to ten minutes from each folksinger. Around the middle of the evening, someone came on stage in a beard, dark pants, white shirt, and a *kipa* (a Jewish skullcap) and started to sing in Hebrew! I didn't know whether he was good or bad, and I wasn't against him because he was so obviously Jewish. What I did know was that he wasn't singing *American* folk music!

I was disgusted! I was at an American folk festival, and this guy was singing in a language I couldn't understand or relate to. Maybe I *was* prejudiced because it was Jewish. Would I have been as upset if someone sang some African folk song in a different language? And yet, on the other hand, that same evening, Country Joe and the Fish sang—and that was also not *folk* music to me. It was in English and they were American, but it was too electric for my definition of folk music. I just wasn't ready to think "outside the box." So much for the opening night.

The next day, there were workshops with many of my favorite folksingers. I stood with my program in hand, looking at a lamppost with all the singers' names written on arrows pointing in various directions. This one to the right, this one to the left. One said "Rabbi Shlomo Carlebach," and pointed over there. I don't know what came over me, but I thought, "Well, what is this stupid guy all about anyway?!" And I went to his workshop.

In a small classroom, Shlomo sat with a few people in front of him. He tried to explain his work in creating American Jewish folk music. After a short time, he said, "Friends, what's the use in talking about it? Let's just sing!" He picked up his guitar and began singing. I don't know how it started, or who started it, but people got up and started dancing, and *I* joined them. He sang, and we sang along and danced around him. And he kept going. At first I enjoyed it, and then my mind started to wander, wondering just how long he was going to keep doing just one song. Then I started to really get into it, but at the same time I was still watching myself, commenting about what was happening to me. Shlomo kept on singing—and at some point the narration fell aside and I felt an ecstatic, uplifting joy and a sense of connectedness. I don't know how long this continued—the workshop was scheduled for only about an hour and a half.

Later, I would look back on this experience through my Jungian lens and describe what happened as my sense of myself—my limited ego, tied and bound in the knots of my socially determined identity—dissolving into my limitless and boundless Soul. I was high on the joy of tasting what it was like to be really free from thoughts, worries, and self-consciousness. But at the time, all I knew was that it felt great.

The next day, after my morning class in physics, I was walking through campus when I saw Shlomo across the street. I quickly crossed over and told him I had been in his workshop the day before, and it had been wonderful. He looked at me with his big, wide, almost bulging eyes. "Why don't you join me tomorrow morning at my hotel?" he asked.

He was inviting *me* to meet him at his hotel! I was honored and excited. The next day, I went to my early morning physics class and then ran over to the Hotel Durant, where Shlomo was staying.

This was a very simple hotel right off campus. Around the corner from a small reception desk was a large room that served as the lobby. I walked in to wait for Shlomo, and discovered that he had also invited eighty or more other people to join him. I was momentarily disappointed; at the same time, I was struck with a very warm feeling to know I was a part of a whole lot of special people. There were men and women, young and old, Jews, African-Americans, Latinos and more. Everyone was waiting for Shlomo, and we waited for quite a while. When he finally came down, he greeted each one of us personally, and then asked if everyone had davened (prayed). I don't think many of us, Jews or non-Jews, knew what he was talking about. He turned toward a wall, put on his prayer shawl and his tefillin, and prayed by himself while we all watched, somewhat intrigued. Then he turned around, asked, "Has anyone had breakfast?" and led the whole group into the hotel's dining room. I don't know whether he had intended to pay for everyone, but all of us assumed he was treating. And he did. He had a bowl of cereal and a cup of coffee, while everyone else ordered "freely" from the hotel's traditional American breakfast menu.

Years later, he affectionately reflected on those days: "Those *hippelachs*, those *dogs*! They even had the chutzpah to order bacon and ham."

He fed us and put some of us up in rooms in the hotel. We never knew how he was paying for this. Shlomo just trusted in God, because he knew he was here to lift up as many fallen sparks as possible.

According to Hasidism and Kabbalah, God made several trial runs before creating the world as we know it today. The first few times, the energy, or "light," was too great for the material "vessels" to contain it, and they shattered. The fragments of the light and the vessels still remained, becoming part of the building material for the next round of creation. But although they were incorporated into our world, they still need to be elevated back to the Source of All Life. Lifting these "fallen sparks" is often called *tikkun olam,* the "fixing or restoration of the world."

And since each person's soul is bound up with those fallen sparks, each of us must do the psychological and spiritual work—the *tikkun*—to discover and elevate our true nature, our true Soul's purpose.

Shlomo touched those broken and fragmented parts within each of us—Jew and non-Jew alike. Shlomo genuinely loved everyone. He didn't judge anyone by his or her outer broken appearance. He only saw the inner holy sparks. Each of us longs to be seen and loved for who we really are—even if we don't know who that is ourselves. We were all drawn to the joy of feeling whole again, even if it was just for the short moments when we were with Shlomo.

Those were remarkable times, with the sweetest feelings of community and love.

Shlomo invited all his "holy hippelach" to a concert he was giving that night at Hillel, the Jewish student center at Berkeley. This wasn't part of the folk festival, and was intended for students and local Jewish residents. The place was sold out, so we waited outside for Shlomo. We waited a long time. He was very late, and everyone was getting very impatient. When he finally arrived, we told him there were no seats left, so he brought all of us up on the stage with him, telling the audience that we were accompanying him. After arriving so terribly late (which soon became his trademark), our presence on stage didn't make the audience any happier.

During the concert, Shlomo told the predominantly adult audience, "You don't like that your children are out on the streets! But, *gevald*! At least they're on the road searching! What are you doing? You're sitting at home. You're not even looking!"

As he started playing and singing, those of us on stage started dancing, and soon, almost everyone joined us, making a big circle all around the auditorium. Not only was the late start forgotten, but the event also went on for hours. If we had danced a lot at the workshop, now it felt like we were beyond time, beyond, in fact, all limitations. The energy, the love, the joy were tangible. The concert was recorded by KPFA, the local listener-sponsored radio station, which ran the tape reels to the studio, so that they were broadcasting the first half of the concert while the second part of the live concert was still going on.

Finally, the Hillel office said it had to close the auditorium, as it was very late. So we left the hall and started dancing outside on the campus quad. Around midnight, we turned on radios and danced to the second half of the concert that was then being broadcast.

It was absolutely amazing to feel so released, awake, and free, and at the same time so contained, surrounded, and embraced in this atmosphere of love. Experiencing so much love from Shlomo, and so much love from everyone else and toward everyone else, was blissful. This feeling of belonging, of coming home, was a taste of the World to Come. It was like the story of the rebbe from Karlin, who had told his Hasidim to get the wagon ready. They climbed in, not knowing where they were going. They rode on and on, beyond any place they were familiar with. But though they seemed to travel greater distances than normal, time was still passing and it was getting later and later. They whispered that it was way past the regular time for *mincha*, the afternoon prayer, and as the sun came closer and closer to setting, they started beseeching the rebbe, "Rebbe, shouldn't we stop for *mincha*?" "Soon," he assured them, but he kept right on going. Then the sun started actually setting, and yet he still answered their pleadings with, "Soon, soon."

Hours went by and they had traveled further than they had ever gone. As midnight approached, the rebbe finally stopped at an old *kretchmer,* an inn. It was as dark inside as it was outside. The rebbe climbed down from the wagon and banged long and loud at the door. At last an old man in his nightshirt opened the heavy door.

"Yes?" he asked.

"We've come to daven *mincha,* to say the afternoon prayers. Please prepare the room."

The old man let them in, and went about his business, lighting candles on the walls and in the chandeliers, and straightening out the tables.

The rebbe and his Hasidism began to pray. Karliner Hasidim are known to daven with every ounce of their strength, shouting every word like their lives depended on it. (They say that many people pray to come back to this world in their next lifetime as an ear, nose, and throat doctor for Karliner Hasidim.)

When the townspeople heard the shouting in the middle of the night, they assumed it was a fire. They jumped out of bed, grabbed a shovel, a blanket, a bucket, anything with which to put out the fire, and came running in the direction of the commotion. But when they got there, they saw that it was a fire, but not the kind they expected. It was an inner, sacred fire. They put down their buckets and shovels, and joined with the others, pouring out their hearts to God.

It was an unbelievable scene, Jews and Christians together, crying out to God with all their souls. And after they all finished praying, the local folks ran back to their homes and brought all sorts of food and drink, and they had a feast that was a taste of Paradise, of the Messianic days yet to come.

Then the rebbe signaled to his followers that it was time to get back in the wagon and return home. Just as he was about to climb up himself, he turned to the old man and said, "Nu? Don't you have something to tell me?"

The old man sighed and said to him, "Rebbe, I'm 107 years old. Exactly one hundred years ago, the Baal Shem Tov came here in the middle of the night with his Hasidim to pray the afternoon prayer. They, too, cried out with all their being until the local citizens came running to put out the fire. Those people also put down their buckets and joined in the prayer, and brought food afterwards for the most heavenly gathering of souls. Afterwards, the Baal Shem Tov put his Hasidim on the wagon, and then he turned to me. I was just seven years old. He put his hand on my head—I can still feel his holy presence—and he said, 'My sweetest child, a hundred years from now, some other Hasidim will come at midnight with their rebbe to daven the afternoon prayer. Tell them ... tell them we were here before!' And then he got up on his wagon and rode away."

"Ah," said the Karliner Rebbe, nodding his head, "that's what I was waiting to hear." And with that, he climbed on his wagon and rode away.

Like these rebbes before him, Shlomo traveled all over the world and had a unique way of drawing so many different people together. When he sang and taught and told stories, it was as if we were transported into a timeless place where we felt so at home and at one, and where we, too, felt we had been before.

I was "with" Shlomo for twenty-seven years. "With" in quotes, because even those who lived near him in Manhattan or on the moshav where he lived when he was in Israel only had limited time with him due to his constant traveling all over the world. So for me, living in California and not New York, and then in Israel but not on Shlomo's moshav, my being "with" him was definitely spaced out. But wherever he was and whoever he was with, there was a timeless confluence of souls descending from worlds beyond and souls ascending from worlds below. At first, I just felt it as universal spirit—

which it was! But over the years it became more and more a powerful Jewish arousal, a merging of our ancient dormant history and our own contemporary waking Jewish soul. Certainly for me, it was the beginning of my spiritual search, of my Jewish identity, of the imprinting of Shlomo as a model and mentor of how to teach and sing and tell stories, and how to travel around the world touching souls. It was just a brief wisp of a glimpse of what I was to become, but there were many more mountains that needed to be ascended and descended along the way before I could even reach toward the highest.

It had been an amazing week of singing, dancing, and learning with Shlomo. We were learning to see people through eyes of love, and learning to be seen through eyes of love, and learning to be filled with *simcha*, with joy. I didn't know this was Jewish. I only knew that it felt right, and that it fit right in with the blossoming generation of flower children.

And now, having just found Shlomo, and having been found by him, he was leaving us to return to his world in New York. But before he left, he wanted to give us some tools with which we could continue the joy we had experienced with him. A core group of us had formed around Shlomo, and we were with him every chance we had. If it wasn't a public event, singing and dancing, it was a private, intimate gathering at someone's home, singing, telling stories, and hearing Hasidic teachings. We had become very connected to one another after spending so much time in a state of joy and love.

But there was really no existing Jewish synagogue or spiritual center that could sustain the spirit and momentum that Shlomo had launched. Still, he told us we had to stay connected. "You have to be Soul Brothers and Soul Sisters to each other," he instructed. "So, how do you do that? You have to become 'Window Brothers' and 'Window Sisters' to each other." We had to look more deeply into each other and let others look more deeply into ourselves.

Then he said, "And if someone spits on your window, you have to turn it into a door, open it up and invite him in!" No matter what someone does to you, you have to find a way to open your heart to *her* pain, to open your heart and allow her into your essence.

The Holy Baal Shem Tov, who founded Hasidism in the late 1700s, said that if we see something negative in someone else, it's really just a reflection of something within ourselves. If my *panim,* my face, is dirty, I'll see a dirty face in the mirror; if my face is clean, I'll see a clean face in the mirror. *Panim* means "face" or "sur-face," and *p'nim* means the "inside" or "the depth." If I'm clean, if I'm pure on the inside, I'll be able to see what is pure within someone else. This is similar to what Jungian psychology calls "projection": we project onto the other what we can't see within ourselves.

Shlomo taught us that even if we were limited and a little unholy ourselves, we could still look more deeply into one another, to see beyond the outer appearances, judgments, and automatic negative reactions. We could see the true holy essence deep within someone else. And doing that would help clear away the impurities and access the holiness within ourselves. We had to see more deeply within each other; we had to let others see more deeply into ourselves. We had to really risk and trust to be windows to each other.

A caravan of cars escorted Shlomo to the airport. We danced circles around him all the way to his gate. Smiling, crying, loving, longing, leaving, we kissed and hugged him good-bye.

After seeing Shlomo off at the airport, I came back to my tiny studio apartment. I hadn't been there much in the last week. I was exhausted from an almost constant emotional and spiritual high and from very little sleep. I called my parents, whom I hadn't spoken to at all during this whole time, to tell them that I'd been spending my time with this rabbi, and it had been incredible. But as I began talking to them, I burst into tears. "I'm really very happy," I explained, "I don't know why I'm crying; I'll call you back in a while."

Sitting on the floor, I tried to figure out what was going on. I realized that all that joy and love had really been generated by Shlomo, and now that he was gone, it was as if it had disappeared with him. It was like standing next to a wood-burning stove in a very cold room. As soon as you stepped away from it, you were cold again.

"I want what he has," I said to myself, "and I don't want to depend on him for it. I want to be able to give it to others, and I don't want others to depend on me for it."

Just like that, and without being fully conscious of what I was saying and meaning, I was reprogramming my life, or perhaps *just* becoming more aware of my Soul's vision and purpose.

I didn't understand it then, but I had encountered the warmth of the fire on the mountain, the warmth of the burning bush. I had to begin to find that mountain and to climb it myself.

Abraham Maslow, one of the founders of transpersonal psychology, referred to the peak experience as "transient moments of self-actualization." When we have a breakthrough, when we reach above the clouds and see the world from a lofty perspective, we are more whole and more self-aware. At such moments, we think, interact, and feel more vividly and more alive than usual. We love and accept and respect one another, have less inner conflict and anxiety, and are better focused in all that we do. For Maslow, the highest peaks include "feelings of limitless horizons opening up to the vision, the feeling of being simultaneously more powerful and also more helpless than one ever was before, the feeling of great ecstasy and wonder and awe, the loss of placing in time and space."[2]

Years later, during my own journey up the mountain, when people in transpersonal psychology talked about their "peak" experience, I used to correct them, saying that, indeed, they had had a very unique experience, but it was only the beginning of the process. It was only a "peek" experience, and that now they must begin the real work of reaching the true mountain peak for themselves.

Shlomo didn't talk about these "peek" experiences, he just took us there. But he did put the whole phenomenon of the psychological and psychedelic revolution in a very different light. "You think you are having such revelations, conscious breakthroughs and reaching such high places because of what's going on in Berkeley and Haight-Ashbury in the 1960s?" he would ask. "I'm telling you, every breakthrough you're experiencing is happening because in the 1967 Six Day War we broke through to the Holy Wall after being cut off from it for so long. Because of *that*, every kind of holiness, insight, and godly high experience is pouring back into the world." It was this peek into that timeless dimension of the Holy Temple that was channeling all the peak experiences that were happening.

4

SHLOMO:
Wash Away Your Habits

Shlomo saw that there was no place for the wandering Jews of the 1960s to go for spiritual fulfillment. So he opened his own place—"The House of Love and Prayer"—in San Francisco. It was a residency for many, a stop-along-the-way for others, and a place to gather when Shlomo came to the Bay Area from the East Coast. One day, when I heard he was coming, I set out to hitchhike from Los Angeles to San Francisco. As I threw some basic things together, I grabbed the book I was hungrily reading at the time, *The Teachings of Don Juan*, Carlos Castaneda's first book which had just come out. I must admit I was asking myself, "Why am I traveling to see Shlomo when I was devouring so much from Don Juan?"

According to Castaneda, Don Juan taught that a man faced four enemies while on the path of knowledge: fear, clarity, power, and old age. First he must fight his fear of learning, of meeting the challenges on the path, until he achieves clarity of mind and purpose. Then the fear falls away. Clarity is the second enemy. It blinds you, making you never doubt yourself, making you think you can do anything you please. Only by knowing the limitation of clarity do you come to true power, which is the third enemy. Power deludes you into invincibility, letting you make your own rules. You become capricious and cruel. With no real command over yourself, and no real knowledge about how to use power, you are used by it. Regarding the fourth enemy, old age—you cannot defeat it. You can only struggle with it until the end.

Don Juan said that the warrior on the path of knowledge must eliminate his personal history because that is who you *think* you are. You learn it from your culture, education, and society, and it prevents you from being who you really are.

When I arrived in San Francisco, I walked into a teaching that Shlomo was giving about Abraham. Abraham had been told by God to "go get yourself from your land, your birthplace and your home, to the place I will show you.... " But it also means "go to your true Self and Soul," because *Lech Lecha*, "go yourself," can also literally mean, "go *to* your Self" (Gen. 12:1). And now, after Abraham's initial journey from his cultural identity to his true Soul, God appeared to him (Gen. 18:1–5). During this revelation, Abraham saw three strangers crossing the desert. "Wait, my lord," he said, addressing the strangers. "If I find favor in your eyes, please don't pass by your servant. Let me bring some water to wash your feet, and then sit under the tree, and then I will bring some bread to sustain your hearts.... "

About this, Shlomo said, "Many commentaries say Abraham is talking to the strangers when he says 'Wait!' But others learn that he is talking to God, saying, 'Thank You so much for appearing to me, but could You wait? Because I really need to feed these strangers coming across the desert.' Then he turns to the three wayfarers and says, 'Please let me help you wash your feet and feed you.'

"You see," said Shlomo, "'foot' in Hebrew is *regel*. This is also the root of the word *her'gel*, which means 'habit.' It is also the root of the English word *regulation*. So, open your hearts to what Abraham is saying to them. He is actually saying, 'Come, let me wash away your *habits*. Then you can sit down under the tree.' And what tree is this? Ah, it's the Tree of Life!

Abraham is saying, 'Come let me wash away your habits. Then you can sit under the Tree of Life, and then I, Abraham your father, can nourish you.'"

There I was, in the House of Love and Prayer, hearing Shlomo giving over the teachings I had just read from Carlos Castaneda. By talking about washing away habits, he was also talking about washing away personal history. The big difference was that Shlomo was learning it from the Torah, and Castaneda had learned it from a Toltec Indian named Don Juan.

5

SHLOMO:
The Words and the Melody

In 1967, I was reading the book *The Puer Aeternus (The Eternal Youth)* by Marie-Luise von Franz, one of the first-generation Jungians. I had met her when I was a boy in Switzerland. She wrote many books on fairy tales and their symbolic meaning. This book was an interpretation of *The Little Prince,* by Saint-Exupéry. She was focusing on the archetype of the youth that never grows up: what she called the *puer.* This included pilots who would not retire at the required age, and then often had fatal crashes, like Saint-Exupéry; or mountain climbers who always had to scale one more mountain before quitting, and often fell to their death.

Then I read "The Puer and the Senex," an article by another Jungian, James Hillman, which carried von Franz's work a little farther. To the archetype of the *puer*—the eternal youth, the Peter Pan who was always determined to experience something new, to never settle down—Hillman juxtaposed the archetype of the *senex,* the old man, fixed and rigid in his ways. For Hillman, these two were different aspects of the same archetype of wholeness, the archetype of process, integration, and completion. One was youthful and curious, always renewing itself. The other, wise and understanding, integrated the new, helping it see its place in the greater whole.

When an archetype first comes to consciousness, it is split into conflicting opposites. The *senex,* the wise old man, doesn't want any new or creative input, and the *puer* doesn't want to hear that this is part of a greater whole. The *puer* rejects linking with the wisdom of the eternally developing tradition, and the *senex* guards his hard-won wisdom and rejects anything new or different or threatening. No doubt my father had given me this book on the *puer* hoping I would come back down to earth after all my high-flying experiences with Shlomo.

This time, with these ideas in mind, I went again to San Francisco to learn with Shlomo. Talking about the Holy Temple in Jerusalem that was destroyed two thousand years ago, he said that we mourn the Temple's loss to this day, but different people mourn different losses. Yes, we lost the daily animal and incense offerings. We lost the role of the holy priesthood. We lost the Sanhedrin, our parliament of wise sages who kept the tradition together and decided how to live and follow the Torah, the word of God. But more than that, Shlomo said, we lost the music that was played in the Holy Temple.

"I want you to know, there were thousands of instruments and thousands of voices in the Temple. It was the most awesome experience to approach the Holy Temple. Between the smell of the incense and the sound of the music, it was beyond. Beyond!"

He explained how the instruments were more complex and advanced than anything we have today. The instruments of India, Turkey, China, and Japan, and the most wonderful classical harps and wind instruments from the West—these only give a tiny flavor of what these instruments were like. The Romans tried to force the Levites to turn over their secrets of music and instruments, but the Levites refused and chose to die rather than let this heavenly art fall into the wrong hands.

"Can you imagine?" Shlomo asked. "Today everyone is selling the deepest secrets of instruments of destruction! Back then, they would rather die than let these powerful musical instruments wind up in the wrong hands.

"But my sweetest friends," Shlomo continued, "worse than losing the musical instruments is that we lost the melodies. The Prophets, when they gave their prophecies, didn't stand on a soapbox and give a little speech! They *sang* their message to the people. Yes, we still have a musical chant for the basic words of the Torah and the Prophets, but it's not the same. Every word of Torah was sung, every psalm and prophecy was sung. When we lost the Holy Temple, we lost the melody to the Holy Torah! We lost its deepest inner meaning.

"The saddest thing today, friends, is that we have an older generation that knows all the words. They know every word, and they guard every word, and they teach every word. But, *they don't know the melody*! They don't know the inside of the inside of the words."

And then Shlomo said, "Today, a whole new generation of young people seems to be so far away from Judaism. But are they? They're moving to a different beat. They hear a heavenly melody. They're dancing a new dance. But, *they don't know the words*!

"If we could just get the guardians of the tradition to listen to the new melody, and if we could just get these inspired young people to learn some of the words, then, like it says in Psalms, we could 'sing a new song to God!' We could really fix the whole world."

Once again, my worlds of Jung and Judaism came back together; the *puer* and the *senex* were there in the melody and the word. Bringing the two together was the healing of our split consciousness. It was the revelation of the lost dimension of the whole Torah. And my words and my melodies were finding their own new and ancient song.

THE WATERFALL:
Going with the Flow

Words and melody. Everything and everyone had its name and label—its word. And deep within, everything and everyone had his experiential existence—his melody—that came from far beyond the limitations of his name and label.

It was a beautiful day in the spring of 1967, and a few of my friends and I decided to search for a waterfall we had heard was in the hills near Pomona's campus. We parked at a turnoff near the winding mountain road. A short distance from the road was a small, wonderful waterfall. We all went our own way. Some hiked, some explored. I sat quietly, closing my eyes.

Right away, the sound of the waterfall and the peacefulness of the place permeated me. "It's so beautiful here," I thought, "and it's just fifteen minutes from campus. I ought to come here more often. It's so relaxing, so calming. I'm surprised more people don't come here.... "

Suddenly, I realized I had stopped listening to the waterfall and was lost in my own meandering thoughts. I pushed the thoughts away and listened to the waterfall again.

Now it was as if someone had turned up the volume of the waterfall. I was "flooded" with the most amazing and breath-taking images of waterfalls from all over the world! There was Niagara Falls, and Victoria Falls, and Tarzan leaping over falls, and so many more. The color, the roar, the mist—it was absolutely incredible. I had never experienced anything like that before. Then I noticed that I wasn't listening to the waterfall. It was an amazing experience, but it wasn't the here and the now of *this* waterfall. Fortunately, I caught myself, and pushing those pictures out of my mind, I again listened to this waterfall.

This time, the volume was more acute, and my head was exploding with every image and sound in the universe related to water: sprinklers, faucets, hoses, and toilets; cars splashing through puddles, ocean waves crashing, rain pouring, and water boiling. There was gargling, splashing, and the plunk of a stone hitting the surface of a lake. I was overwhelmed with these images and sounds, but abashed that, once again, I wasn't listening to *this* waterfall. As before, I pushed those images out of my mind, and returned to this waterfall.

Now, it was really roaring. What I heard was like an orchestra. I could hear a whole symphony, or distinguish each separate instrument that was playing its part: every swish, rush, and swirl of the gushing water itself. It was like entering a microcosm of the waterfall's sounds. This heavenly symphony was quenching my thirsty soul; the universe was bursting into song. Then I realized that as lofty as this seemed, my mind was still putting one more illusion between me and the waterfall.

Returning to listening, really listening to the waterfall, I started to shake a little, thinking, "*This* is what meditation must really be about!" Then I said to myself, "Will you shut up?! Stop observing yourself! Stop patting yourself on the back! Just listen to the waterfall!"

And now there was a thunderous roar, and a blinding white flash, and the waterfall came roaring right through me. For a timeless moment, I was "one with the waterfall." Almost immediately after that came the thought, "Wow, that was incredible. That must be what it's *really* all about." With that, I returned from my brief encounter with the Tree of Life, and returned to the Tree of Knowledge, to my busy mind of opposites and dualities. But it had touched my soul and left an eternal impression.

From then on, whether or not I was able to penetrate all the layers of my mind to see or hear something or someone, at least I knew for certain that there was so much more than I could perceive at the moment. In fact, that became my best working definition of mysticism: There is so much more than we can know.

That waterfall was one the most significant meditation teachers I ever had.

7

ALAN WATTS:
The Sound of One
Hand Clapping

I don't know whether it was a blessing or a curse, but I felt like I was strongly rooted in both the theories I was learning and the experiences I was having: the words and the melody, the *senex* and the *puer*. I wasn't rejecting one for the other. But it was still a challenge to put them together, to get them to "talk" to each other, to make them whole. I had an understanding of what the soul is and had experiences of it. But how could I access the soul more easily? How could I maintain that elusive presence of my soul in the every day? Could I get to the roar of the waterfall again—and not just in the waterfall? Could I sustain it? Could I reach that level with people and sustain it? Who knew? Who could help me?

It was a privilege growing up with Jungian mysteries, myths, and maps of these relatively uncharted inner worlds. I knew that Jung had the experiences, studied the ancient spiritual maps, and put them together; he lived them, practiced them, and taught them in his own unique way. I was too young to have done extensive long-term Jungian therapy, the inner work that can go on for many years. I didn't know whether Jung's followers went as far in their own self-exploration as Jung had, or whether some of them had gone farther. I think there is a natural tendency in all systems—psychological, philosophical, religious, spiritual—to fall back on the intellectual study and mastery of the maps, without necessarily pursuing one's own inner experiences, or risking pushing the envelope of the ego *too* much. I was looking for more.

On the other side, lots of people were having all kinds of deep meditative or psychedelic experiences, but without the maps and grounding of the psychological or spiritual traditions. Many of the pioneers in Eastern meditation, like Ram Dass, talked about reaching great heights, but in the end they "came down" to their fragmented, everyday personality with all its problems and neuroses. Many of them began doing the psychological and therapeutic work, admitting that meditation was not a substitute for it.

Shlomo just took me there, but he didn't talk about the maps, or what it meant to our psyches or consciousness. He just took you there.

So, now that I had *my own* personal experiences and some exposure to the charts of this still less traveled road—my Jungian maps, my Shlomo spiritual breakthroughs, my psychedelic experiences, and my meditative revelations—I needed to figure how to put it together for myself. And I didn't want to just stumble or "trip" or dance or "chance" into these higher realms. I wanted to learn how to gain access to them at will. And I wanted to be able to make that feeling of wholeness, of integration and integrity, more and more my true nature. I wanted to *live there*, not just visit there.

Around that time I started reading books like *The Way of Zen, The Joyous Cosmology,* and *Psychotherapy East and West,* all by Alan Watts. I also went to some of his lectures. Alan grew up in England in the 1920s. As a teenager he had already written articles on Buddhism, and later he studied theology and became an Anglican priest. In the mid-1930s, he moved to the United States and got more and more involved in Eastern studies and practices, explored LSD, and wrote extensively on how he integrated these worlds. When I met him in 1967, he was often at gatherings with Timothy Leary (the former Harvard professor and pioneer of LSD), Ram Dass (the Harvard psychology professor originally named Richard Alpert who explored LSD with Leary and then went to India for the spiritual component), Gary Snyder (Zen/beatnik poet), and Alan Ginsberg (beatnik/Buddhist poet). Their dialogues were enriching, exciting, and challenging.

I met Alan when he spoke at the Claremont Colleges. I was enthralled by what he said, but more importantly, by how he said it, and even the "timing" of when he gave the "punch line," or main point. He did it in a way that bypassed the logical mind and went straight into your heart and consciousness. Watching him present a teaching was like watching a bowling ball slowly roll down the alley. You think you know where it's going, when suddenly it hits a different target, driving home a point that was quite unexpected. Watts surprised you so cleverly, so adeptly, that the knowing could slip into your heart. Then he would laugh—such a hearty laugh—at catching you unawares, at unknowingly leaving your mind behind.

That was exactly what I was looking for. I heard that Alan was going to be in Los Angeles, giving a very exclusive seminar. I crashed it, challenging him about pricing himself beyond the range of students (like me) who really needed and appreciated his message. Without batting an eye, he said, "Come up to Sausalito and attend the summer seminar on my houseboat for free!" Talk about verbal martial arts! He took my words of attack to stop me in my tracks and invite me into his home.

In the summer of 1967, I called Alan, reminding him of his invitation. He told me to come an hour before the seminar started to sit at the door and collect people's payment. That would be my volunteer work for the seminar. I was there early and stayed late each time, for the month-long series.

I recall him talking about the Chinese word, or calligraphic character, for *crisis*, and saying it was the same character for the word *opportunity*, because every crisis is an opportunity. He wanted to draw the Chinese characters and began working the solid block of ink in a flat dish with a little bit of water to make the ink the right consistency. That took quite some time. Then, he took out a brush, and rolled it gently around in the ink. All this took much time, and eventually Alan said, "If you were angry with someone and wanted to write an angry letter, it wasn't so easy. By the time you made the ink, and prepared the brush, and laid out the paper, most of the anger of the moment had been 'dissolved' into something more accept-able."

He spoke so eloquently about the importance of discover-ing who you really are, and of meditative practices that help you find that out. But more important, he talked about chang-ing the way you think, changing, in fact, your very thought process. In *The Book: On the Taboo Against Knowing Who You Are* he wrote:

> The feeling of being lonely and very temporary visitors in the universe is in flat contradiction to everything known about man (and all other living organisms) in the sciences. We do not "come into" this world; we come *out* of it, as leaves from a tree. As the ocean "waves," the universe "peoples." Every individual is an expression of the whole realm of nature, a unique action of the total universe. This fact is rarely, if ever, experienced by most individuals. Even those who know it to be true in theory do not sense or feel it, but con-tinue to be aware of themselves as isolated "egos" inside bags of skin.[3]

He talked about it, experienced it, and helped others feel it, too. Getting to know Alan—his warmth, his humor, his pres-ence, and his humanness—was a special gift.

During that same summer, I had a number of very signifi-cant meditation experiences. These yielded deep insights, and I felt the separation between my ego and the universe fall away. I called Alan on the phone, and, in my youthful enthusiasm, proclaimed, "Alan! I know what you're talking about!"

He could have said, "What gall! What chutzpah! Who do you think you are?" Instead, he said, "That's wonderful! Why don't you come over and tell me about it?"

35

No judgment, no doubt, no seniority. No saying, "I don't have time for this." Just joy and acceptance and patience.

On the way to Alan's houseboat, I stopped at a market to pick up his favorite—Raineer Ale. It was a warm, sunny day and, when I got to his home, we sat outside and talked for a long time, sipping our cool ale.

I told him how I had reduced my meditation experience, and its accompanying insight, down to its essence: it was about discovering that we aren't *lost,* separate, alienated individuals. Rather it was about discovering, *finding,* that we are part of a greater whole—"the One," or "God," or call it whatever you want. All this has been hidden away from us. And although that knowledge and experience of our true nature is the essence of all the verses in all of the ancient spiritual teachings, those verses have been lost—in understanding if not in actuality—and need to be found again. I told Alan that I had the perfect title for the book I would write about my "enlightenment"—*Lost Verses Found on Lost Versus Found.* The title really said it all. The rest was commentary for those who couldn't get it directly: how to find the lost verses of ancient scripture that explained how to deal with being lost versus being found.

Alan laughed warmly and said he always wanted to publish a book that was just a list of the titles of the books he would never write. People could contemplate the title and get the full depth of the consciousness within each one. I remember that one of them was titled *Zen in the Kitchen.* In fact, I have often referred to that "book" of Alan's when talking about the consciousness of keeping kosher—not just the *laws* of kosher cooking, but the conscious intention, the "soul of the mitzvah."

8

"THE EXPERIENCE OF SELF-DISCOVERY": Integrating My (Remarkable) Meetings

It was the fall of 1967—my fourth year at Pomona College. I had been called in to the dean's office a few times; sometimes it was about my grades, sometimes about my antiwar activities. The deans knew that while I was politically active, I was always approachable, never sought confrontation, and constantly tried to keep communication open.

I didn't know why they had called me in this time, but the dean of men and the dean of women were both there. This looked serious. The dean of women said, "We need to know what it's like being stoned."

Innocently enough I answered, "I don't know what you're talking about!"

"We don't want to bust or arrest anybody," she answered. "But we are responsible for the students who drive up to the fraternity cabins on the hills for an evening of drinking and smoking. We know what it's like to be drunk and how drinking can affect driving and what risks that entails. But we don't know what it's like being stoned and how smoking affects your driving. Please help us so we can arrive at a reasonable policy about these activities off campus."

I gave them as much information as I could, from my own limited experience, and it seemed to help relieve their concern.

Some time later, I was again called in to the dean's office. Again the two deans were there. What could it be this time?

"There have been drug conferences on a number of campuses," they said, "warning students of the dangers of drugs—physically, psychologically, and mentally. We would like to have one here, and we would like you to coordinate it."

"You've printed everything from those conferences in the school paper," I said. "Everyone already knows the dangers. Many students think it's still worth the risk." I paused, collected a few thoughts, then said, "Most people want to pursue these experiences because it takes them beyond their ordinary selves. You don't need another conference on the dangers of drugs. You need a conference that offers alternative ways—other than drugs—to have these kinds of experiences."

"What do you mean?"

"A conference that would bring in meditation teachers from all sorts of traditions: swamis, Zen masters, rabbis, and priests who can teach meditation practices for people to try out. I'd bring in psychologists experienced in sensitivity training and group dynamics to lead groups for students who want to break through their outer personalities. I'd bring in Jungians to talk about dreams. I'd bring in street poets from Haight-Ashbury and creative dance therapists who would take students out of their heads through movement. I'd organize several weeks of opportunities to experience the Self. Only after the experiential part, would I bring in philosophers and spiritual teachers for the 'conference' segment of this event. They would put all this into an intellectual framework."

If I could, I told them that I'd have truckloads of snow shipped in from somewhere, just so students would wake up in the morning to a totally different reality: the idea was to *delight* them or *wonder* them out of their regular mind-set.

They considered all this for a minute, then asked, "What would you call a conference like this?"

"I'd call it 'The Experience of Self-Discovery.' But we won't gather to talk about the experience. We'd gather to experience it!"

"Well," they said, "go do it."

And so it began. We came up with the ideal teachers and speakers, including Alan Watts, Shlomo Carlebach, Carl Rogers, Jungian psychologists, and a time frame for the two phases—the experiential and the theoretical/conference. We drew up a budget and began inviting people. But it wasn't so easy.

Year after year, the college had put on large conferences focusing on topics such as Red China or urban development. Each was funded by generous grants from major corporations. But when these corporations heard that this conference would not specifically be *against* drugs, they refused to sponsor it. It was too much for them to understand. We now had no outside funding.

But there were a lot of miracles. The first was that the college even wanted to hold such an unusual, ahead-of-its-time conference. The second was that the college wanted to proceed even after outside funding disappeared. The third was that although we lost a few of our teachers who needed fees, most said that this conference was so unusual that they would come anyway. All they asked was that we cover their travel expenses. The spirit that the idea evoked was remarkable. It really was an experience of self-discovery for everyone.

When the conference finally began, students sang and danced for *hours* with Shlomo. Under the guidance of Carl Rogers's staff from the San Diego area, many sensitivity training groups were held. Anna Halprin led exhilarating large group "dance" sessions. There were meditation lessons, and dream workshops, and San Francisco street poets read from their work and encouraged students to write their own free verse.

I opened the conference segment, quoting Bob Dylan, "He not busy being born, is busy dying." For speakers we had a Zen master, a swami, and a range of psychologists and philosophers.

For me, this was an amazing opportunity to put together everything I had been learning and experiencing outside academia and bring it to the campus. It opened doors of perception for many students, faculty, and administrators. It was an experience of self-discovery. But I didn't get the snow.

9

GETTING HIGH OR GETTING TENURE: Idea-Man or Fact-Man

A few weeks after my first experience with Shlomo, I was at my first party in Berkeley where people were smoking marijuana. Of course, I'd heard about it, but I had never tried it. Now I did, and was pleasantly surprised to discover that I didn't have to do Hasidic dancing for hours to achieve a euphoric feeling. I continued to use it for a while, but soon realized its shortcomings and limitations.

Lots of substances and weekend workshops can take you *out* of the "slavery" to your socially approved personality and into some sense of freedom, but those shortcuts usually won't get you *in* to the "Promised Land." As Crosby, Stills, Nash, and Young sang, "You who are on the road must have a code that you can live by." And yes, some people take substances as an authentic spiritual or religious ritual. But for me, after a number of very special, spiritual, and filled-with-wisdom-and-awe kinds of experiences, I knew I had to reach these through natural means of meditation, prayer, psychological work, song, and dance. I knew that I had to find my own way to inner balance. I saw how easily people could depend on these externally induced agents, and how, after coming down, all the basic psychological work remained for them to resolve in order for their new insights to be real and permanent.

I have been eternally grateful that my first "high"—dancing for hours with Shlomo—occurred so naturally and spontaneously, in a spiritual context, and not just for the sake of getting high and feeling good.

I was beginning to understand, through various teachers, books, and experiences, that it is *experience* that opens the understanding of the heart and mind. All the learning from the best of teachers and books is not as powerful as experience. I *understood* things very differently after each new experience. *When* I was able to transcend my ego, which was bound by time and space, *when* I was able to experience the breadth and depth and all-inclusive Godly-Life-Force or Soul, *then* something changed little by little and in a permanent way. Sometimes it was a change in a mannerism or an expression of speech. Sometimes it was more subtle, coming in small, barely perceptible changes.

As a result of an experience, I might then read something and have a totally different understanding than someone else would have—even a scholar in the field—because I *knew* it *experientially* and, in a sense, *exponentially*.

I remember writing a paper for a comparative religion class on the Buddhist concept of the *Alaya Vijnyanna* (the Storehouse of Knowledge). This concept speaks of a dimension of existence where all knowledge is stored and accessible for any individual who can reach it. I thought my paper was very insightful. I got a "C" on it. When I asked my professor why, he said, "Zeller, you're an 'idea man.' I'm a 'fact man.'" He wanted dates and references to other authors' explanations, not my own ideas from my own experiences.

Later, sitting in the student union café, with a stack of religion books in front of me, someone I'd never met approached, pointed to the books, and asked how I liked the comparative religion course. I mentioned how the teacher wasn't very deep and how he didn't like what I had written. "I know that professor," this student said. "He knows religions like a tourist. He's visited them from the outside. He never lived any of them." I looked at him, and suddenly I knew: "You're his son, aren't you?" "Yes," he said, "and I was with him when he visited those world religions.... "

I learned there really is a difference between experiential learning and book learning and that not all teachers understand or appreciate that difference.

But how does one acquire this consciousness? Hasidic teachings provide us with the shortest, simplest, and most natural way. Extensive study of mankind's wisdom and poring over its tomes of knowledge will not bring us to this desired level. The only way we can achieve it is by simply devoting time every day to meditating, quieting and clearing the mind of all distraction and focusing our attention. Only through personal practice can we reach these levels of consciousness.[4]

10

Dr. Ho and the *I Ching*

In another one of my attempts to bring together Jungian psychology and Eastern studies, I walked into the Asian studies department, looking for someone who might know something about Chinese philosophy. I was directed to Dr. Ho. I found him sitting in his office—an unassuming older Chinese man. He politely asked me to come in, and offered me a seat. I explained that I had read just about everything written about the *I Ching* in English and that, coming to it from a Jungian perspective, I was interested in writing a paper on the archetypal themes of basic hexagrams and their images. I told him I would like to find someone who could steer me toward some original Chinese texts relating to the subject.

"I have studied this a little," he said. "Maybe I can help you."

He tried to clarify how much I knew and determine how I had worked with the book in English. Finally, he said, "I have perhaps the largest collection of books on the *I Ching* outside of China. Maybe you have some friends who would like to study this. We could make it an official class and learn about it from the original sources."

I was dazed. I had hoped to find someone who had simply heard of this esoteric book. Now I found someone who lived and breathed it.

With four friends, we were able to form a course. For an entire semester, we got a glimpse of the complexity, the clarity, and the depth of this "book." It was so much more than a book.

And it wasn't used so much for divination, as I had thought. Rather, it was a book of wisdom, to be studied and internalized in order to understand the way these archetypal patterns flow in history, in current events, and in our own personal lives. With Dr. Ho, we learned the *I Ching* from the inside. It was like studying chemistry and learning how different chemicals react when brought together. We depended less on the English translations and worked directly with the lines, the hexagrams they formed, and the interactions between them.

We also discovered that Dr. Ho was quite advanced in tai chi and in acupuncture, as well as in humility. What a gem, this quiet and unassuming old man.

One day, I asked Dr. Ho where he lived; he indicated that his home was a few miles from campus. "How do you get here each day?" I asked.

"I walk."

"But it's so far."

"It gives me a chance to get my thoughts together for the day."

I offered to pick him up and he agreed. He had a nice suburban house that the college had provided him. Outside it had a fairly typical garden and trees. But inside it was not at all typical. It was almost completely unfurnished! The kitchen was almost bare.

"Are you living alone? Are you managing okay here? Are you getting enough to eat?"

"I am doing fine, thank you. It's just that my wife always took care of everything. I miss her very much."

Apparently, Mrs. Ho was still in Taiwan, waiting for a visa. "How did you meet?"

"It was an arranged marriage."

"You married her without knowing her?"

"Over the years, you get to know and love each other."

At that time, I still knew nothing about arranged marriages in Judaism or in India. Even *Fiddler on the Roof,* that classic Broadway play about traditional Jewish life in the shtetl, with its stories about arranged marriages, was just a fairy tale to me.

On another occasion, I asked whether he had written any books himself.

"In China, you don't write a book until you're over sixty years old."

"Why is that?"

"When you're forty, you think you know something, and you write your book. Then twenty years later, when you have perhaps really gained some wisdom, you write your *real* book. People pick it up and look at it and say, 'Oh yes, I remember him. He wrote a book many years ago. It wasn't so good.... ' And they put it back down. So we wait until we are older before writing our own book."

That conversation had a big effect on me, and it gave me the strength and patience to wait many years before writing. I hope it's okay to be writing now.

11

Waking Up *to* Israel

The idea of studying in Israel came from Yehezkel and Rivka Kluger, two Jungians who were quite knowledgeable about Judaism and who actually practiced it. They weren't just Jewish Jungians. They were Jungian Jews: the real connecting bridge between these two core parts of my identity. They were very close friends with my parents, and every year we had a Passover seder in their home. Their Jewish and Jungian commentary, their songs, and their joy and pride in being Jewish were very significant to me.

Our Jungian seder explained that our true inner Self has become enslaved to the pharaoh of our ego, our controlling, dominating personality. Only by standing up to the ego can we break the stranglehold that our superficial identity has on our true Soul. And even after becoming free, it may take forty years in the wilderness to really reach the Promised Land. Those forty years were compared to "the process of individuation," the Jungian term for the long therapeutic process of coming into your true Self. It wasn't until I met Shlomo that I learned that Hasidism talks in very much the same way about an individual's awakening.

Yehezkel, in fact, was my first therapist. When I was having trouble with my grades the first year in college, my parents thought that some inner work might help. My sessions with him were very warm and supportive, and we talked about everything going on in my life—from Pomona and particular courses, to growing up in general, to dealing with my parents and their worries about how I was doing in college.

And we worked on my dreams.

Once, I had a particularly lucid dream: Giraffes were gracefully eating leaves that were very high up on a tree. Almost like a narration over it, a voice was saying, "The God of Abraham, Isaac, and Jacob is coming." It was peaceful and reassuring, but I had no idea what this was about. Yehezkel felt that just as these giraffes could draw down nourishment from beyond the normal reach, this dream was telling me that I had the ability to drawn down spiritual nourishment from a place beyond the reach of my rational mind. There are higher sources of nourishment for our soul, and we have an undiscovered part within ourselves that can reach all the way up there. "The God of Abraham, Isaac, and Jacob is coming"—and that was *before* I met Shlomo!

A few years later, Yehezkel told me about a new overseas program at Tel Aviv University and encouraged me to apply. Still, at this point, I wasn't going to Israel for the pursuit of my Shlomo-awakened Judaism. As a Jungian child, I knew I had to deal with my own spiritual roots before legitimately going on to explore other spiritual traditions and practices. I was going to Israel in order to leave it, and go further East.

I hadn't the vaguest idea what to expect in Israel. When I went shopping for any special items I might need for my year-long stay, all I knew was that it was a desert. I bought very good sunglasses, and I almost bought a pith helmet!

Arriving at Lod Airport in Israel, I felt for the first time in my life that I was really outside of Western culture. Foreign language, foreign-looking people (not just European), a foreign climate. It was hot and muggy at night (very different from Los Angeles). There was a general lack of American efficiency and cleanliness. I eventually found my suitcases and went searching for a taxi. It was already quite late at night.

My taxi driver welcomed me. "Is this your first time in Israel?"

"Yes."

"This may be the Holy Land," he said, "but don't expect to find any holy people!"

That was my official welcome. I guess I had arrived.

———————

This was the first year of the Tel Aviv University's overseas program, and they weren't quite ready for us. Instead of putting us up in a dormitory on campus, they put us in an old hotel, very far from the campus, on the beach of Hertzlia, just north of Tel Aviv. It was like no dorm I had ever lived in. For that matter, most of the students were like no students I had ever dormed with. First of all, except for brief times with Shlomo, I had never been in an almost totally Jewish community. And anyway, with Shlomo, many of those around him were from all religions. Second, I was a graduate student, and most of these students were freshmen and sophomores. And finally, most of these students were pampered and spoiled; some had even brought trunks filled with such essentials as American soft toilet paper and "can't-live-without" kinds of food from home, including chocolate and peanut butter. All I had were my desert sunglasses.

It was hard being so far from the campus and being bussed back and forth every day for our Hebrew language *ulpan*, the Israeli special intensive four- to five-hours-a-day course for learning Hebrew in a couple of months. Every day we went from total Hebrew immersion back to our English-speaking colony. But it was wonderful being right on the beach, where I took many long walks, collecting my thoughts and many seashells. I loved the sea: swimming in it, walking along it. It was a good transition from my upbringing along the Pacific.

———————

Still, it was a great relief when we were sent for a three-week "kibbutz experience" when the *ulpan* was over. My group was sent to Kibbutz Palmach Tzuba, a small kibbutz half an hour west of Jerusalem. Our living quarters were the wooden cabins from the kibbutz's early days. They had their share of wear and tear, and it could properly be said that they had been demoted from cabins to shacks. The wood was very weatherworn; each cabin consisted of two rooms, each with its own entrance from a front porch, which was shaded by an extension of the roof stretching over it. Mattresses stuffed with straw lay upon simple metal-frame beds. It was all very basic. Surrounding the cabins were a combination of trees and lots of weeds. Many of the Americans in our group actually cried over these barren conditions. I was so happy to have such simplicity and—except for their crying—such peace and quiet.

Though I had not done any hard physical labor while growing up, nor was I very sports-oriented, I took to my work assignment, digging up weeds from an overgrown field, with great enthusiasm. I really can't explain it, but I relished the work. I actually enjoyed getting up at 5 a.m., putting in an hour or two of work before going to breakfast, then returning to the fields. And I was so proud of my kibbutz work clothes an boots! After all the years in college in boots and blue jeans and work shirts, the uniform of the leftist student activist, I was really working! One of the kibbutz members had to remind me that after work, they all changed into regular clothes.

Along with being given specific work assignments, we were also assigned a family to whom we could go every day after work. Most students went into Jerusalem, or hung out in their rooms, rather than connect to their families. For me, the work was a real high, but higher than that was the family-centered gatherings after work. I loved my Israeli family. I visited every day and was welcome. This family time was sacred! No one would come during this late afternoon family time to discuss work. That had to be taken care of at the communal showers right after work, or later in the dining hall.

Amnon and Ahouva Magen were my "parents." They had several children; the oldest was in high school and the youngest was in kindergarten. Amnon was short, tough, and wiry, and had a big mustache. He drove heavy tractors and large trucks. Ahouva was petite and delicate and worked in the laundry. But she had held many other jobs in education as well. Both had fought in the Palmach, the pre-statehood army, in the Israeli War of Independence in 1948. They were also active in the administration of the kibbutz. Amnon was the talker and the storyteller. His English was quite good, so until my Hebrew improved to conversational levels, we spoke in English. Ahouva was more on the quiet side, mainly focused on their beautiful children; she always had great cakes and cookies waiting for us.

The two of them were absolutely wonderful, kind, and constantly welcoming. Back then, there was no television in the homes on the kibbutz, just one in the social hall. We listened to the radio, read books, and *talked* to one another; and in good weather we might walk around the kibbutz.

The children had their own dormitories where they slept with their peers in a different part of the kibbutz, and although it appeared they were more separate from their family, they actually spent more time together than most families in America. I began to learn that kibbutz life is very dynamic and alive. Two years later I was to see this really from the inside, when I worked in organizational development for the kibbutz movement.

Just as I had learned the maps of our psyches from Jung, but arrived "on location" by dancing with Shlomo, so it was with espousing the hip values of simplicity and cooperation. For me, it was on the kibbutz that I really got beyond the "talk the talk" to "walk the walk." I once mentioned to Amnon that I missed the radical gatherings on campus where we argued the politics of socialism and communism, workers' rights, unions, demonstrations, and more. He said, "We don't talk about it so much. We just live it."

The kibbutz taught me about the pyramid of values that placed the survival and security of the country—Israel—first; the viability of the community second; the family third; and then the need of the individual. Though some people gained personal prestige from leadership or rebellious roles, most prestige came from family. People seemed genuinely to work to live, not live to work. And still, they loved the work. Hershel, another kibbutz member, shouted over the roar of his tractor that plowing was like making love with the earth. This was a slight variation on what Rabbi Kook, a great mystic and the first chief rabbi of Israel, once said when comparing the furrows in the plowed ground to the indentations left on the arm after wrapping tefillin.

I learned to love my neighbor as myself, and to do unto others what I would want others to do unto me. I learned to love Israelis. And if I'm at home in Israel today, I owe much of that to being made to feel so at home on my kibbutz and with my family. Though I don't see them often enough, I have maintained contact with them and visit them with my family from time to time.

12

How Saddam Hussein Made Me More Jewish

Life on the kibbutz was wonderful. The kinds of work I did, and most important, the different people I became close to left an indelible impression on my heart.

One day, I went to visit a new yeshiva in the Old City of Jerusalem. It was built upon the ruins of older buildings that had been destroyed in the various battles over the city. Things were very makeshift and temporary. If I thought the conditions on the kibbutz were simple, the yeshiva took that word to a whole new meaning: somehow, it ran on a broken shoestring—and on a lot of trust in God.

I told the rabbi at the yeshiva that I had been turned on to Judaism by Rabbi Shlomo Carlebach, that I was now living on a kibbutz and was interested in exploring the possibility of learning at the yeshiva. He asked if I was staying on a religious kibbutz. I didn't even know that there were religious kibbutzim, and, anyway, despite the two years since I had met Shlomo, I was still not keeping Shabbat or keeping kosher or practicing any other religious observances.

My kibbutz may not have been religious, I told the rabbi, but the way the people lived and worked together and shared everything, and their values of equality and commitment, made it the most "religious" community I had every experienced. He was not too happy with my response, and he was worried about the kosher conditions at the kibbutz. I didn't understand much about the laws of keeping kosher or their meaning. About all I knew were the basic laws of preparing kosher meat, and about cooking meat and dairy in separate pots, and not eating them together. But to me, the kibbutz, in general, and its kitchen, in particular, were so clean—compared to most other places, even kosher places—how could there be a problem? If a chicken is raised in inhumane conditions, but it is ritually and humanely slaughtered, does that make it kosher? Is kosher but unclean so much higher than unkosher but clean? That wasn't where I was at. It's probably why, soon after, I became a vegetarian. So I stayed on the kibbutz and nourished those values that were more important to me then; and, for the time being, I didn't pursue the yeshiva.

Midway through the year, I woke up early one morning and turned on the radio, just like every Israeli: the news was paramount to us. The newscaster reported that Iraq had executed nine Jews for allegedly spying for Israel. In a closed trial, they had been convicted and, already, they had been hung in the streets. Thousands of Iraqis were dancing around their dangling bodies, shouting for joy. It was awful to hear and I quickly turned off the radio.

Later that day, not feeling well, I went back to my room and laid down. I thought maybe I had the stomach flu or a virus. I turned on the radio for the afternoon news, and again heard the report from Iraq. This time, I almost threw up. I realized I wasn't sick with the flu. I was sick to my stomach—literally— by identifying with those Jews in Iraq.

I felt the hatred that so many people had for Jews. I knew that it could just as well have been me hanging in the streets of Iraq, or wherever. For the first time, I realized I wasn't just "born Jewish." Being Jewish wasn't just an intellectual choice. It was deep in my *kishkes*. I had marched and protested over the treatment of so many other people in the world, particularly for African-Americans back in the United States. I had been active, often a leader, in the civil rights and antiwar movements. My compassion for the suffering of others was real and palpable. But

I had never felt that *my* life and the lives of *my* people were on the line. That may seem foolish just thirty-five years after the murder of the Six Million, including all my grandparents. But that was my reality, a very naive reality.

When I realized that my illness was a visceral response to my identity as a Jew, I fasted for three days as a way to focus on this experience. I wrote letters to my parents and to other Jewish Jungians who had fled Germany in the 1930s: "After what you suffered just for being a Jew—not even for being religious—how could you go to America? How could you stay there, instead of going to Israel?" I got some very deep, soul-searching answers from them. One Jungian answered that she had come to Israel, but left after dreaming that something in the earth was poisoning her children. She took it as a symbolic statement that something in the collective mentality of the young Israeli society was poisoning her creativity. And so she moved to the United States.

Shlomo had touched my soul; Israel and the kibbutz had touched my heart and my body; now this had touched my *kishkes*. Yet, I still had no clue that, eventually, I would become religious and come to live in Israel.

13

THE LIZARDS:
Touching the Earth

The more I worked on the kibbutz, the more I came down to earth and felt my roots plunge deeper and deeper into Israeli and Jewish soil and soul. I was digging up tall weeds in the field and stomping down cotton as it was picked and dumped into large cagelike wagons. I worked in the baby chick hatchery that smelled like scrambled eggs. I helped a cow give birth—it took three or four of us tugging with all our strength to pull this calf into the world. I loved the contact with growing things, from cotton to fruit trees, and even more with all kinds of animals.

After a day's work, I loved sitting out on the porch of my cabin, enjoying the sun. The lizards also loved the sun.

I would sit very still on the porch floor and look at a lizard. He was also very still, and very close. He would look back at me. I felt sure there was eye contact between us. After a while, we would close our eyes, as if to say, "I trust you so much. I'll close my eyes, knowing you won't do anything against me while I'm not looking!" After a while, we'd open our eyes just to see what the other was doing. If we both opened our eyes at the same time, we'd close them again right away. It was very peaceful and harmonious.

After a while of building trust, and feeling more and more present, I'd put my hand on the wooden floor, close to where the lizard was sitting. We both remained very still and maintained eye contact. Slowly, he climbed onto my hand, hesitated briefly, and then continued up to my shoulder, where he would sit for a long time. My hair was wet from showering, and he enjoyed the cool, safe shelter.

As a child, I used to make eye contact with our pets—our cats, rabbits, and parakeet. It was special to do this with such a "simple" creature like the lizard. I believe that beings of different levels of creation can interact and communicate. I had learned about this in a book my father had given me when I was younger, *Kinship with All Life*, by J. Allen Boone. Years later, Carlos Castaneda wrote about this, and I particularly remember his description of the lizard as a creature that communicates between the human and the spirit world.

The kabbalistic model of the Four Worlds teaches that all life comes into being through God's "Emanation (Will)," "Creation (Plan)," "Formation (Construction)," and "Action (Completion)." This applies across the board, from the "Big Bang" through evolution; to a seed disintegrating and growing into a tree; to a "seed-thought" of an individual going from idea to plan to action to "fruition." It is also expressed in the progression from mineral to vegetable to animal and to human.

To me, the *interaction* between those worlds—for a human "being" to contemplate upon a rock, to commune with plants and trees, to communicate with a wide range of animal life, to form community with people, and to do it all with love for all of creation and for the Creator—is the most miraculous of all. I understand this to be a major fixing or restoration, a vital healing that takes place when we humans interact consciously with the other worlds of creation.

14

THOMAS BANYACYA: Hopi Spokesman and Interpreter

After my year in Israel, I returned to the U.S. for graduate studies at the Claremont Theological Seminary. After my experience with "the Experience of Self-Discovery," the coordinator for an upcoming conference on American Indians at Pomona College asked me to help out however I could. The subject greatly interested me and I was happy to make myself available. As it turned out, there wasn't a lot I could do for the conference, but there was something I could do for one of the presenters.

Thomas Banyacya, official spokesman of the Hopi people, had been to Washington D.C. and the UN many times on behalf of various Hopi causes. He was not a medicine man or tribal elder; rather, he was their ambassador to the outside world. His most important role was telling about the Hopi prophesies. The prophesies were based on very old rock drawings and oral transmissions from the elders that told of the ancient past and depicted the future that was yet to come.

When the prophesies were first given, over a thousand years ago, many of the signs just didn't make sense: You will know the time is coming when the land is covered with spiderwebs, or when there are rivers of solid water stretching across the land, or when the tops of the trees are dying. And they told of a small container that could spread fire and destruction and illness over vast areas.

Thomas Banyacya's job was to communicate to the world how the elders translated or interpreted those signs into events that were happening now. He explained them quite clearly: the spiderwebs are telephone and electric lines; the solid rivers are paved highways; the tops of trees are, in fact, dying from air pollution; fire and destruction was the nuclear bomb. These things had been seen in visions, hundreds of years ago, but who could understand the images they saw? Their visionaries could only describe what they saw in images they knew from their own everyday life, such as spiderwebs, rivers, and the like.

Thomas was soft-spoken, unassuming, and very committed to telling his people's story. The elders mainly lived in their own world and culture; Thomas had to walk and communicate in both worlds. He wore a Hopi shirt with thin, colored ribbons woven into it, a red scarf headband, and Hopi jewelry around his neck. One sign that he was a "traditional" Indian, not a "modern" one, was his long hair.

One story that Thomas told during the conference at Pomona was that, originally, there had been two tablets of stone with ancient drawings-as-teachings on them. The tablets had become separated from one another. The Hopis still possessed one of them, and in the future their long-lost people will come from the east with the other tablet and they will be reunited. I was fascinated by Thomas's story of the ancient tablets. It had such a Jewish reverberation.

He described how Native people were here to keep the land holy and clean through prayer, meditation, ceremonies, and fasting, and that a spirit in everything and in all people guides us, helping us do the right thing and steering us back on track when we stray. He warned that the "white brother" was wandering farther and farther away from the spiritual path, and that the path of materialism took people very far from the spirit. I remember that in the middle of his dramatic talk in the large auditorium, all the electricity blew. We knew it was a sign.

Thomas apologized that he would have to leave the conference early. The Hopi's springtime ceremonies were about to begin, and he had to be with his people. This ceremony was their participation in the Creator's process of bringing new life out of seeds that have lain dormant, deep in the cold ground, throughout the winter. A short time before, members of each clan had planted some beans, and at the end of the springtime rituals, the men would leave their kiva (their clan's sacred, underground ceremonial space), and go up and out—like a plant growing out of the ground—and distribute these first sprouts to the village women. This was a ritual of renewal and new growth, and prayers were offered for the transition from winter to spring weather.

In fact, Thomas said, he could really use a ride from Southern California to his village in Arizona. I jumped at the opportunity. Afterward, he explained that most of his travel arrangements were handled by God, who made things work out to get him where he was supposed to go. You might say he got to places "as the Spirit moved him."

The drive to Arizona was beautiful, with much time for conversation and getting to know each other better. It was early spring, and it had been a pretty dry winter. There really was a need for more rain. The sky was a clear, deep blue. As I drove, Thomas explained that the Bean Dance, which was integral to the springtime ceremonies, was ordinarily closed to the "white brother," and that while usually the members of the different clans come to their ceremonies in full costumes and masks, in the Bean Dance they perform without masks. One reason for this, he explained, was that spring is a time of new beginning, and we only take on our masks in life as we grow up. Now, as young sprouts, we don't need them. Also, because the Bean Dance initiates children of the proper age into their clan, the adults are without masks so they can be recognized.

With clear skies and clear highways, we arrived just in time. To my delight, I was invited to descend into the kiva to witness the dance and the ceremony! The chanting they did while dancing was variations and combinations of the sounds *"Ya-ha-way-hey-ya-ha-way-hey-ya-hey-hey."* These were the sounds of the Hebrew letters in the *Tetragrammaton,* the four-letter name of God! Again, there was a feeling of an ancient Jewish connection. I was just waiting for the two tablets to be reunited.

At the end of the ceremony, when we emerged outside, to our wonderment the sky had filled with dark clouds and it was snowing! The weather had totally transformed. This reminded me of one of Jung's favorite stories about the Chinese Rainmaker. My father said that on various occasions, Jung would ask, "Did I ever tell you the story about the Rainmaker?" And everyone would say, "No, we never heard it! Please tell it to us." And he would tell the story once more:

> There was a terrible drought in a region of China. Crops were failing, animals were starting to die, and it was getting more and more difficult for people to survive.
>
> When someone said they heard about a Rainmaker in a distant province, they agreed to send for him at once. Surely he could save them. When he finally arrived, days later, they pleaded, "Please help us. Tell us what to do and what you need so you can bring the rain."
>
> "Please provide me with a small hut," he answered, "and leave me alone."
>
> He went inside. Outside, everyone waited with considerable anxiety and great anticipation. One day went by, then two. When would he come out? On the third day, clouds started to gather and it proceeded to rain.
>
> "You did it! How did you do it?"
>
> "Me? I didn't do anything," he said, "You see, I come from a region where everything is in harmony. It rains

in its season, and the sun shines in its time. All is in peaceful balance. But here, all was in panic and disarray, and when I entered your chaotic space I was pulled out of my own alignment with harmony, with the Way of All Life. So I needed a space where I could meditate and return myself to harmony. When I am back in balance, everything around me can return to the flow and balance of life. Now we are all in *Tao*, and if rain is lacking, rain will fall, returning everything to the *Tao*, the Way."

Judaism has many community practices—prayers, fasts, repentance, charity and other good deeds—that deal with drought and similar phenomena. Yet, here too, the tradition tells the story of Honi HaMa'agal, the individual righteous person who sat inside a circle he drew around himself, and called on God to bring the rain. And it rained.

You can decide for yourself whether the Bean Dance had anything to do with this change in the weather. For me, there was no doubt about the cause and effect, of going deep within to reconnect with the "way" beyond.

15

HARRY:
Running Away to Home

Early 1970: the phone rang. It was my good friend Steven Westbrook. He had picked up an interesting hitchhiker on his way from Los Angeles to Claremont, and wanted to bring him over to my house. He came in with a young teenager, neatly dressed in slacks, a white shirt, and a black hat, and with just the beginnings of facial hair, hinting at a future beard. He had a paper bag under his arm. My friend said that when he picked him up at the on-ramp to the freeway, he had told him he was heading to New York. Steve wasn't Jewish, but he'd been exposed to a wide range of traditions while growing up. He had sized up this young teen as a religious Jew and figured that the paper bag contained his tefillin. The young man seemed quite innocent and naive, and Steve felt that he may not really have understood how far it was to New York, how many days it could take, how "unkosher" it might be between Los Angeles and New York, and frankly, how dangerous it might be to hitchhike that far.

Steve brought him to me because I was Jewish, spoke some Hebrew, and after my experiences with Shlomo Carlebach, he thought the boy might relate to me. How this boy might perceive us—Steve and I were both long-haired, bearded hippies—hadn't occurred to him. We decided that I would try to distract him with "Jewish" conversation as long as I could, while Steve would check whether he was a runaway: strict laws forbade helping or forcing a minor across state lines.

The hitchhiker had shy, gentle eyes and the sweetest smile, and when we asked him his name, he smiled and said, "I wish I could tell you, but I can't." In the meantime, we said, we would call him "Harry," which seemed all right with him. He was worried about being prevented from continuing his trip, or being sent back to Los Angeles, and kept asking us to bring him back to the freeway. We explained that we wanted to help him, but we needed to know whether he was running away from home. He would only say that he was not running from home, but rather *to* home. He'd been sent from New York to Los Angeles to be a camp counselor for the summer. His parents thought it would be good for him to get some California sun. He was miserable and wanted to go home. He knew his parents wouldn't be happy about this, so he was doing it on his own. Once we had established that he wasn't a runaway, Steve began phoning all our friends to raise enough money for a plane ticket to New York for "Harry."

"Harry" told me he lived in a religious community in Brooklyn. When I asked what it was like to keep Shabbos, he looked at me with surprise. "What's it like *not* keeping Shabbos?" he said. It was inconceivable to him. That answer touched me deeper than anything I had ever heard—or would ever hear—about Shabbos.

Returning from his phone calls, Steve gave me a wink. Again, Harry asked us to take him to the freeway. We explained that, instead, we would take him to the airport so he could fly home safely. We had even located someone who was going back to New York who would fly with him to see that he arrived okay. Our friend would even put him in a cab at JFK Airport, so he could arrive in Brooklyn in style.

As I watched Harry react to all this, I wasn't sure if he was simply accepting what was happening, or if he was *expecting* a miracle from God. I didn't know what he had prayed for that morning before setting out to hitchhike to New York. All I know is that *we* were blown away by our encounter with this boy, literally from another world, and how moved and impelled we felt to help him get back home.

But that's not the end of the story. Several days later, someone called asking whether I knew anything about a missing boy. When we checked for reported runaways, we had called from both the campus religious center and the campus counseling center to various centers in the Los Angeles area. At the time, there were no reports. But now that someone was reporting a missing boy, they told him of our inquires. Through the counseling center, he got my name, and was calling me for information about his missing boy. Now it was *my* turn to worry about saying too much about myself. I told him this must be a mistake, because the boy I had helped wasn't missing. He was home in New York. The man said the boy he was looking for was not at his home in New York. I said we put him in a cab from the airport! He asked whether we could meet so he could show me a picture to make sure we were talking about the same boy. He assured me he was not involved with the police. He just wanted to know in which city he should be looking for the boy.

A little nervous about what might be the consequences of our actions, I met the man that night. He showed me the picture. It was "Harry." The man, who turned out to be "Harry's" uncle, was very relieved, and thanked me and said at least now they knew where to look for him.

The next day, his parents had located Harry. It turned out he was afraid to go home because they would be mad. So he went to his Brooklyn yeshiva and hid in the library and was living off of candy bars.

A week later, I got a letter from his mother, thanking us for the mitzvah of getting him home safely, and asking for the cost of the ticket so she could reimburse us. I tore up the letter. No one was going to take away our mitzvah.

Now, more than thirty years later, I wonder whatever happened to "Harry." I just want to let him know what happened to me, and that I keep Shabbos now, and that I wonder about all those people who don't.

16

FROM ISRAEL TO INDIA: Finding My Way Back Home

After my year on the kibbutz, I had become fascinated with "intentional" communal experiments. I read many books on the history of communes in the U.S., and since this was 1970, hippie communes were springing up all over the country. I visited some of them and found they had the ideals to live together and share everything, and often, *everyone*. The kibbutz members, in addition to their ideal of Jews returning to work the land and their love of the work, had an extra magical ingredient: it was their love of working the land—the *"Land* of Israel"—that was so inspiring. On the communes, there was a love of being on the land, maybe an identity with American Indians. But I don't know whether there was a love for the "land of America." While pursuing my interests, I heard of a group that was doing work with kibbutzim back in Israel. I was curious about what they were doing and went to interview them. Instead, I was interviewed by them.

It turned out they had brought several members of different kibbutzim to study in certain American universities that offered programs in organizational development—O.D. for short. O.D. had developed within business schools as a way to integrate group dynamics, communication skills, problem solving, conflict resolution, and goals clarification. Its purpose was to boost efficiency and productivity, determine the spirit, meaning, and purpose of an organization, and then share this with all levels of management and labor. It had been a great success in large corporations like IBM. Now this great idea was being applied to the kibbutz. Several managers of kibbutzim were going through this graduate program in the States, and soon a whole team of O.D. specialists would be sent to Israel to apply their trade directly to a few kibbutzim.

The U.S. team had much experience in dealing with American corporations, but virtually none with kibbutzim. And the Israelis had much experience with kibbutz life, but virtually none with O.D. and corporate America. Neither side knew the other's language.

I fell between these two groups. I had experience with group dynamics, having spent several months with Carl Rogers's staff during my senior year in college, when I ran the "Self-Discovery" conference. And I had spent a year on a kibbutz, where I'd acquired a working knowledge of Hebrew. So, although I was a long-haired hippie—fitting into neither of their worlds—I was asked to join their team and help bridge their different cultures, values, and languages.

In our usual Western lifestyles, we live several separate and usually totally unrelated lives—family life, work life, social life, and maybe a religious life, but they are all separate and independent of each other. And it's unlikely that anyone in one world knows me in any other world.

But in kibbutz life, there are hardly any boundaries. The wife of the person you work with is your child's teacher. If there is friction at work between the two of you, it could very well cause friction for your child. And so it is with the people in the kitchen, or the people who arrange the work assignments, or the people who assign cars for particular outings off the kibbutz.

It's one very big foot, and no matter whose toe you step on, it's your toe. And so I came on board to help in this exciting experiment with organizational development in the twenty-four-hours-a-day kibbutz model.

The kibbutz leaders really wanted us to help solve their problems: intergenerational gaps, work conflicts, and communication issues. A big one was that kibbutz management and leadership needed to be handed over to the next generation, but the founders found it hard to let go of their power and control. It was very hard for them to grasp that one way to solve the larger, community-wide problems was to work on their own personal problems. On top of that, the Israelis came from many different kibbutzim and from different political movements and ideologies. This separated them. A common refrain was, "I can't let my kibbutz's problems be known to members of other kibbutz movements. This is none of their business."

Bob Tannenbaum, the head of the project and a professor at UCLA's School of Business, was incredibly patient, understanding, kind, and gentle with all of us on the team, and especially the Israelis. He was very skilled at handling their fears, resistance, and blind spots, and he had a gift for seeing into the true nature of a problem. Indispensable as well was his ability to laugh *at* himself and *with* others and to keep all of us going through some very intense processes.

The American team was only in Israel for the first couple of months, during which we trained more people at a kibbutz training center, then worked with them on a few of the participating kibbutzim. When the rest of the trainers returned to America, the kibbutz members who had been through the training and I worked with several other kibbutz communities. Getting to know a kibbutz this way, discovering the ideological conflicts behind the scenes, shattered many of the idealistic and romantic impressions that I had from my previous kibbutz experience. But I still loved and honored the people and their way of life.

I did O.D. on various kibbutzim for a year. Looking into the deep inner workings of what made a kibbutz tick made me take a much deeper look at what made me tick. I realized that before I tried to guide other people in living their lives, I needed to work more on my own.

It was then that I met Allan Shapiro, who was visiting Israel after having spent some time in India. His descriptions of life in India—the culture, the people, the spirituality—were enthralling and *inviting*. Allan talked about crossing the border into India and feeling that you were in a basically vegetarian country. He spoke with his wide, smiling eyes, his mouth in the biggest, happiest grin, and his arms gesticulating with great animation. When I told these stories to others, they would ask me details about India and I had to explain that I had never been there; I had just heard these lively descriptions.

In my two years in Israel, I'd had very strong experiences that confirmed the depth of my identity with this land and its people. But other than Shlomo, I still hadn't found my way into Judaism as a religion. Eager to feel and taste the holiness that I knew was deep within, I began to make plans to continue my spiritual journey, this time further East.

17

Sri Pad:
Only God Brings
You Here

Allan returned to India and sent me several letters while I was still in Israel. He was at an ashram in Vrindavan, a small town between New Delhi and Agra, where he was studying with a guru who had given him the name Asim Krishna Das. Asim means "the infinite," and Krishna Das means "servant of God." I set out from Israel, first flying to Greece to see my parents, who were on their way, in a roundabout route, to Zurich for the summer. Then I flew to Turkey, where I formed a band called "Cranberry Sauce" to while away the time until the Shah reopened the borders to Iran and I could begin hitchhiking to India.

I was going to India with the intent of visiting Allan briefly. After that I planned to go on to China. India seemed too crowded with followers of gurus who had made it big in the West, like the Maharishi of Transcendental Meditation and the Beatles, and the Hare Krishna movement. I wanted what was different and uncommon. China was the land of the *Tao* and the *I Ching*. I had studied these in depth. The way of the Jungian, they were the source of the Fire on the Mountain. But this was 1971, and I would learn that China was still essentially closed to the outside world. I would soon find out that there was enough mystery to be discovered in India.

I went to Vrindavan, looking for Allan. I finally found him walking across a field. I ran over to him and we hugged joyously.

Then he looked across the field toward a scraggly haired, bare-foot Indian man wrapped in a faded, Army-green blanket.

"Oh my God!" Allan exclaimed, "That's the most 'hidden' guru around. Very few people have any idea how holy he really is!" He ran over and threw himself at his feet.

This guru wasn't even wearing a white or orange cloth, and he didn't have flowing white hair—all of which I thought were the signs of a holy man. But I walked over anyway to greet him.

"It is a very great honor that you have come to Vrindavan," he said, "for only those who God brings come here."

"Oh, no!" I said, "I knew Asim from Israel. I had his address."

"Yes," he said, "lots of people have addresses, but only those people whom God *personally* brings come here."

Though I thought I had come here of my own volition, he was trying to shift me to a different kind of cause and effect. He was introducing me to a *separate reality*. (I remembered Shlomo saying, "Lots of people have an address, but so few people have a home.")

His name was Sri Pad (pronounced "Shree Pod"), which means, "The Blessed Feet [of God]." He was a sadhu. Sadhus don't live in ashrams or, indeed, in any kind of religious institution. They usually live outside and bathe in rivers; whatever they have—food, clothing, temporary shelter—comes from God. The sadhu lives from the Hand of God. Most of us fool ourselves into thinking we are in control. The sadhu way of life helps him realize that only God is in control and we are totally submissive to Him.

Sri Pad's English was excellent—one of the positive benefits of the former British Empire. He turned to Asim and asked, "Why don't you bring your friend to the *leela* this evening?" Then, turning to me, he motioned toward my boots. "We take our shoes off whenever we enter a holy place," he said. "In Vrindavan, every place is holy. So why don't you just leave your boots here in a nearby ashram where they'll be safe?" That was the last I saw of my boots. I remained barefoot until I left India, a year later.

The main form of entertainment for the people here were plays called *leela,* with musical accompaniment that acted out the main stories of their religion. These were usually family productions, with families carrying this on from generation to generation. They started very young, playing simple instruments and working with various props. Then they took on the major roles in the play. As they got older, they became more accomplished as musicians or got more involved with costumes and props; as that occurred, the elders would become the directors and conductors. There were two productions in town: one for the "common" people, who flocked to these plays in droves as we might go to the movies, and one for the spiritually elevated, the gurus and priests of the community. I was privileged to be invited to the latter.

The play was beautiful, with its sets, costumes, music, and acting. It centered on a heroine who was searching for her lover, who had disappeared. It was a metaphor for each person looking for God, who is hidden from us. She went everywhere, asking, "Have you seen my beloved?" Everyone replied that he or she hadn't seen him. I was appreciating the play from an artistic perspective. But as I looked around at the audience, I saw that they were all crying: they'd totally identified with the woman's longing for her beloved. For me, this was excellent entertainment; for them, it was reality. Once again, I was seeing that there is a separate reality of God, and that every "drama" and trauma in our life is God's *leela,* God's cosmic play.

Sri Pad had arranged for me to sleep in someone's home. Most people lived in simple one- or two-room dwellings. There was no electricity, only candles. There was also no gas for cooking; some people burned wood, but most used dried cow dung. And there were no toilets; a narrow canal or gutter ran along every "street." People went to the bathroom there, covering themselves with their cloth shawls for modesty and privacy. A few times a day someone from "the sanitation department" washed the waste away with water.

The "home" I stayed in was actually a space between two dwellings. My host, Gun'sham, had put a roof over the open space and a wall in the back. This was home. The truth is, his home was like a temple, and everything he did was a service to God. Though as poor as could be, Gun'sham managed to provide me with the basics of bread, tea, and a blanket at night. He did this with total love and with total joy. He knew that everything in his life was a gift from God, and that whatever he gave anyone was going straight to God, since we are all manifestations of the Divine. His whole life revolved around serving God.

Most people wore a dhoti, a long cloth very elaborately folded around the legs and the torso; others wrapped a more simple cloth around their waist, with maybe a long, loose shirt for a top. Sri Pad remarked that I must be very uncomfortable in my pants, and he took me to a tailor for a length of cloth. He also had me measured for a long-sleeved Indian shirt. I had lost my shoes. Now I lost my clothes.

Sri Pad and his small group of followers, mostly from the West, were up long before me, bathing in the river and going to early morning meditation. Later in the morning, I usually found them at one of their meditation stops, and joined them for the rest of the day. Soon, Sri Pad asked if I wanted to stay with them, sleeping outside, and joining them from early morning. This was a big step to really becoming a sadhu, and it was probably the last thing I thought I wanted to do. But I couldn't admit this. So I said that I couldn't do it because I didn't have a blanket of my own.

I don't know where he went. Or whether he went anywhere. It seemed that Sri Pad just turned around and suddenly was handing me a plaid blanket. Now I had lost all my excuses and was being introduced into the way of a sadhu.

Bit by bit, I was losing my "Western-ness." Nobody was demanding this of me. I did it because it felt so comfortable, and because I felt so much at home. I did it because it was being offered by people who were so loving and so caring.

18

NEEM KAROLI BABA AND RAM DASS: Be Here Now

The word was out that Neem Karoli Baba was in town. He was the guru of Ram Dass, the author of *Be Here Now*, which was a delightful collection of wisdom and graphics, reflections of his experiences with LSD, and, more important, his spiritual discoveries and transformation through meditation and spirituality.

Vrindavan was Neem Karoli Baba's winter home, as it was too cold at that time of year for him to remain in the Himalayas. He had become well known to many Americans because of Ram Dass, formerly Richard Alpert, a psychology professor at Harvard who had experimented with LSD. Ram Dass had eventually gone to India, where, among other things, he realized that LSD had little effect on people who had achieved enlightenment through meditation and other spiritual disciplines.

When Ram Dass first met Neem Karoli Baba, the dialogue went something like this.

"You have medicine for me?" Ram Dass didn't understand what he meant. "You have pills for me? Give them to me!" Ah, Ram Dass now understood. So he gave the guru a tablet of LSD.

"Give me more!"

"No, one is all you need."

"Give me more!"

He gave him another.

"Give me more!"

Baba swallowed the LSD all at once. As Ram Dass waited for the guru to feel the effect of the drug, Babaji sat calmly, looking into his eyes. Rather than Neem Karoli Baba tripping, Ram Dass's mind was blown as he realized that there were worlds and dimensions where LSD could never take him.

Baba was known for his pure and generous heart. He was always saying, "Love everyone. Feed everyone." Well, I had lots of love, but the "feed everyone" sounded real good to me. In fact, when I got to his ashram, though he was giving a talk, he knew my heart's desire, and sent me to the kitchen to eat, rather than hear him. After I finished eating, I met with him. It was a brief meeting, as if he knew I had Sri Pad for my guru, and that I had come to him for the food. He was very warm and kind— an old man, wrapped in his blanket. But his smile was that of a child, filled with love, innocence, and delight. He asked where I was from and where I was going, but he probably really wanted to hear whether I knew that I came from God, and whether I was trying to get back to God. And even though I still answered more geographically than theologically, saying I was from California and would eventually go back there, he gave me his blessings that my journey should take me to God.

Soon after, we heard that Ram Dass had come to Vrindavan to see his guru. I had heard Ram Dass talk a few times when he had participated with Alan Watts, Timothy Leary, Gary Snyder, and Allen Ginsberg at several "high" symposiums in Haight-Ashbury. In Kabul, the crossroads of East and West for those hitching to India, there was a restaurant called Siggy's where news and tips about traveling, border crossings, and tough border police were available. His book *Be Here Now* was being passed around. In the courtyard of my humble hotel, I read the book in a single sitting. It really spoke to my heart. And now, Ram Dass was here in Vrindavan.

Sri Pad asked me to bring Ram Dass some *prasad*, some holy food. He was staying in a simple guest house/hotel. His room was small and dark. It seemed he wasn't feeling well. He was so happy to receive the gift, and it seemed to really lift his spirits. That was my first personal encounter with Ram Dass. Little did I know we would maintain a personal connection for the rest of our lives.

19

Sri Pad's "School for Sadhus"

Like Asim and Ram Dass, a lot of Westerners were becoming Hindu, or surrendering to their gurus. Many even planned to live in India for the rest of their lives. From my experiences with Shlomo and Israel, and my Jungian dedication to do justice to my own tradition, I was pretty sure that I was not going to go in that direction. Yet I also knew that this was an incredible time in my life, that some alchemical process was accelerated by being in this foreign culture and tradition. But I also knew, in the end, that I had to go back to my Jewish destiny.

I had to tell Sri Pad that *I* wasn't here forever. But what if he was upset or angry? What if he thought that I had led him on, or deceived him, or used him? What if he told me to leave, to stop wasting his time? When I found him, he was sitting alone on the steps in front of an old temple. I approached him, fearing the worst, bracing myself for rejection.

"I'm not planning to become a Hindu," I told him, "and I don't plan to spend the rest of my life here!" This insistence to do things my way wasn't so simple. In the back of my mind was the fact that I hadn't surrendered to him, or to anyone else before him for that matter. I didn't become religious for Shlomo, and I wasn't becoming a Hindu for Sri Pad, and I didn't get my PhD for my father. Was this a healthy sign of positive ego strength and Jungian-style individuation—the ability to stand up and make my own decisions in the face of social or religious pressure? Or was it a sign of weakness and fear of taking the plunge and letting—no, *trusting*—someone else tell me what to do, to guide my soul? Why was I always calling my own shots? For me, this is a constant debate along the psychological and spiritual path.

I prepared myself for the worst, when he said, "Time and place have nothing to do with God Realization. You're here? You want to work on yourself? You want to come closer to God? Let's get to work!" His smile, his warmth, and his full unconditional love were still there for me. He had no attachments or agendas, no personal needs. He wasn't keeping score of how many devotees he had. He confirmed that I had to make my own decisions.

My sadhu "training" continued. I learned to have fewer possessions, and I detached myself from a Western daily schedule that typically revolved around mealtimes. When I had left Israel for India, I had packed very consciously, keeping everything to a minimum. I ended up with a medium-sized backpack and a small shoulder bag. Instead of bringing my guitar, which was too big, I had brought my silver side-flute, which took up little room in my backpack. Now here I was in India, and the flute and its case were too big for my small sadhu shoulder bag. I put it aside for a small, light bamboo flute. Other than that, all I had was my blanket, my passport, and the clothes I wore—a dhoti-wraparound; a shirt; a plain, soft, pale yellow cotton shawl called a *chumbel;* and a smaller all-purpose cloth that could be a turban, a neck scarf, or a simple wraparound to wear when bathing in the river (because you were always covered for modesty). I also had a journal, a small inspirational book with teachings of different Indian holy teachers, and some cash for an emergency.

As a sadhu, I didn't even carry a begging-bowl for eating or drinking, as many monks did. I learned to cup the flat round bread, chapatis or rottis, like a bowl in my left hand so it could hold potatoes, rice, vegetables, or lentils that might also be given with the bread from whoever might be feeding me. Then

I would tear off a piece of the bread with my right hand, wrap it around some of the vegetable, and eat it. I learned never to put my left hand (that's the toilet hand) to my mouth; and once my right hand had been to my mouth, I never touched anyone with it until I had washed after the meal. I couldn't even touch the handle of the water pump with that hand until I pumped some water with my elbow and washed my hands. Otherwise, I would have technically contaminated the whole well.

I was learning to trust that God would always provide. If there was more of something, fine. If there was less, fine. If there was nothing, I'd guess that we were fasting. One day, while getting accustomed to this attitude, I ate at a temple where they fed us sadhus a meal, and I put a few extra chapatis in my bag, "just in case." Later that day, we were invited to a special religious feast where there was more delicious food than I could possibly consume. There had been no need to stash the extra food. There was only a need to trust in God's Providence. Like I said, I was learning.

Another time, Sri Pad sent me on an unusual lesson about being detached from food. He had seen me look longingly toward a passing wagon that was loaded with delicious bowling-ball-sized clumps of brown sugar, called *gur*. "Oh," he said, "would you like some *gur*? I'll send you to where they make it, and you can have as much as you want!"

He told someone to take us there, and to tell the people there that he had sent us. They welcomed us warmly and said they would show us the whole process, starting with the sugar cane and ending with the brown sugar balls. We came to a place where a water buffalo, attached to a long wooden pole, was walking around in circles, operating the cane "juicer."

"Here, we feed the cane into the machine, which crushes them and gives the raw sugar syrup." He gave us a large piece of sugar cane, saying, "Here, start with this. Strip it with your teeth and eat it right from the cane. It's delicious."

He walked over to the cane "juicer" where the syrup was flowing into a large vat. He took a large earthen cup to catch some of the syrup, and handed one to each of us. "Here, drink this!" I was still trying to finish the cane, and he kept filling my cup with more syrup, which was very filling.

The vats with the syrup were put over a fire and boiled. The clear, whitish syrup turned into the brown sugar. He scooped some out for us to taste. "See the difference in the taste and texture? Here, have some more!"

There was still one more step in the refinement process before it was rolled into the balls and sent to the market. Again, he gave us a large amount of the *gur* that we had been eyeing so hungrily just a short time ago. "Here, now you have the finished product. Here, have some more!"

I felt sick to my stomach, overdosed on sugar in every form it can come in. I had lost a lot of my things over the weeks in Vrindavan. That day I lost my appetite for brown sugar—*gur*.

I never knew where or from whom my next awakening would come. One day, I was talking with friends in front of an Indian temple. The image of us American sadhus discussing deep cosmic ideas evoked images in my mind of Greek philosophers in their togas, debating ultimate Truth. It was hard not to be a little self-conscious and slip out of the present. No sooner had my mind wandered than a skinny, little Hindu man walked by. He paused and cocked his head, as if to listen to our discussion that was going on in English. Then he turned to me, gave me a gentle whack on the forehead, and said in Hindi, "Radhé, Radhé, Radhé, Radhé, Radhé." Or, "God, God, God, God, God!" Then he walked away. I realized that he was saying, "Stop talking about God. Experience God!"

Another time, I was doing "holy work," *sadhana*, in a very sacred walled-in garden. This garden was a place where mystical events took place at night. It was an extraordinary privilege for a Westerner to be allowed in there at all, let alone to do this holy service. What was I doing? You see, the stones of the walkway got very hot during the day. So when the garden was closed to the public at the end of the day, I had to carry bucket after bucket of water from the well, and pour it onto the stones to cool them down. That way, any visitors who came from the heavenly realms at night wouldn't burn their nonphysical feet.

As I worked, I tried to stay focused and present. This was service that got no acknowledgment: no one would see me and no one would thank me. I began to think how holy it was to do this, how unique. And then—whack!—a low tree branch hit me in the forehead! That was a painful and rude awakening. My mind had wandered. Lost in my wonder, I was quickly brought back to the present moment.

But I had come to India to see other places beside Vrindavan. I approached Sri Pad about this. He wasn't my master or my guru. I hadn't surrendered to him, but I did defer to him. He was my wise teacher. I said, somewhat awkwardly, "I appreciate so much how you've taken me in, and I'm learning so much. But I really came here to travel. I'm not really sure why I'm asking you. But ... can I go?"

He looked at me, surprised, and said, "You're free to go anytime you want. No one is keeping you here! But next week, there's going to be a special music festival, with some remarkable Indian classical musicians. It would be a shame to miss it."

I stayed the week. It was no ordinary concert: these musicians were really performing just for God, not for public fame. The music was incredible. I was so pleased that I had stayed.

Shortly after that, I again went to Sri Pad and said, "Thank you so much for telling me about the music festival. It was beautiful. I'm so glad I stayed, but, uh, can I go now?"

He responded as before, "You're free to do whatever you choose to do. I'm not holding you here. But tomorrow is a very special holiday, and you might want to stay for that before you go."

Again, I stayed. And again, it was a very moving and beautiful experience.

This happened a number of times, and I began to get the feeling that every day was special, even if nothing out of the ordinary was happening.

Late one night, and early in my initiation into sadhu life, Sri Pad announced to a few of us that we had to leave right away to catch a bus for Ghoverdan Mountain. I had no idea what that was, or where it was. With fewer and fewer possessions, getting my things together on short notice was no problem. We headed out on foot—barefoot—to the outskirts of town. Everything was closed except for one tea shop. Sri Pad asked the *chai-wallah,* the tea man, where we could get the bus to Ghoverdan. "A bus to Ghoverdan? At this hour?" he laughed. "There are no buses anywhere this late at night!" He waved us away and shut down his shop.

Five minutes later, out of the black night, a bus pulled up. The door swung open, and the driver called out, "Ghoverdan!" Without batting an eye, Sri Pad stepped on board and motioned for the rest of us. We were astounded. We were on our way. I just didn't know to where.

Hours later, the bus came to its final destination. We got out and Sri Pad started walking. It was so dark that I could hardly see a step ahead of me.

Walking barefoot during the day is hard enough. But at night? Forget it! It was impossible. I tried my best to pierce through the dark, straining my eyes to see sharp rocks or thorns. I would spot one—or at least what I thought was one—and step over it, only to land directly on a real one, and it really hurt. Or I'd make out the dark round shape of a cow "patty." I stepped over what turned out to be a shadow, and stepped into the real thing!

If that wasn't bad enough, all my tension and fear gathered into my ankles, which started swelling from the stress. And my footsteps were getting heavier and coming down harder. I wasn't going to last much longer. This was the night I learned to pray. "Please God, help me! I can't see where I'm going. Please make him stop for the night."

As if God were answering me, I realized that this was no different than walking through life in what I think is clear broad daylight. I think that I see something coming up ahead, and make various moves to avoid it, and invariably, I walk smack into the very thing I'm trying so hard to avoid. I can no more control and determine the things happening in my life than I can control and determine where to place my next step in the dark. In fact, I'm *always* in the dark, even in the light. I'm almost always psychologically unconscious, no matter how physically alert I may be.

I understood that I needed to let go of my desire to control, predict, and direct my life, and even to control my next step in the dark. I needed to turn over the reins to God. If I could simply let go of the illusion that I could do things better myself, I just might get myself out of the way, and there would be no telling what I might reach or where I would be guided.

So instead of looking down, I looked ahead or up. My ankles relaxed and my step lightened. I let my feet do the walking, this time at a slow, more natural, more graceful pace.

The difference was remarkable. It wasn't that I stopped stepping on stones or thorns. But when I did, my step was so light that they couldn't penetrate. It wasn't that suddenly there were no cow patties. But my step was so light that I felt the change of texture under my foot. Now my steps glided over a patty without sinking in.

What a difference! The change had happened so quickly. Then, almost as quickly, Sri Pad announced we were stopping to rest until morning. My prayers were answered, practically and symbolically: I didn't have to go on like this anymore.

The next morning, I felt like I was radiating from the breakthrough of the previous night. I was different, free, liberated from some lingering old mind-set of how to "plan ahead." Sitting and meditating in the warm sun, I thought, "I must be crazy. I'm having the most transformative and insightful experiences—right here and now—and I've been bugging Sri Pad about leaving. Now, I don't want to go anywhere."

We were sitting on some steps by a pool of water. It was a beautiful, bright day and Sri Pad was reading to us from the teachings of holy men like Ramakrishna and Ramana Maharshi. Sri Pad said, "Oh, his teachings are so profound. Why, even the place where he lived is especially powerful and beautiful." Then turning to me, he said, "Yes, you'll see it soon when you start your travel!"

"No!" I shouted. "I don't want to go anywhere. I just want to be here with you!"

"*Now!*" he said. "Now you are ready to see India."

Without ever saying, "How can you see other places when you aren't even able to see where you are now?" Sri Pad had led me to my own awakening. He began telling me where I should go and who I could stay with. He gave me the India he had journeyed through, the families he had stayed with, the ashrams he had gone to. He gave me an ancient, spiritual India that was removed from the modern world. He gave me India on a silver platter.

He told me that although when he made his spiritual journey, his *yatra*, the buses, trains and boats were always there for him just when he needed them, it wouldn't flow quite so seamlessly for me. Doors might not open quite so promptly, and I would have to do some waiting along the way.

And with that, he *sent* me away!

20

The Calcutta Rabbi

Being a sadhu in the countryside was very different from being in the dense city of Calcutta. First of all, people in towns and in the countryside tended to be more religious, so they really accepted a sadhu as a religious person. Whereas in the city, sadhus were suspected of being beggars. Also, it was easier to find solitude under a tree and away from people in the rural areas, and there was less worry about getting sick from the food because the religious homes and temples were very strict about washing food. But most unsettling was that the place Sri Pad had told me to stay didn't let me in, and now I had to fend for myself.

I saw on my map that there were a few synagogues in Calcutta. I figured it couldn't hurt to check them out. Though I was living as a sadhu, I still had my love of Judaism and Israel. Besides, the rule of thumb for a traveling Jew anywhere in the world is: go to the local synagogue and they will take care of you.

Barefoot, with a cloth wrapped around me, and hair down to my shoulders, I walked into the synagogue. Someone dressed in Western clothes was sitting there, studying from a book. He was wearing a yarmulke, a skullcap.

"Shalom!" I said. "I'm a Jew from America and Israel, and I really need a place to sleep."

He said he was the rabbi, and that I could sleep in the synagogue. When he learned that I hadn't eaten, he took me to a small restaurant down the road. Over dinner, he was quite curious about my adventures and how I came to be where I was.

When we returned to the synagogue, he said, "I've studied pretty much all Jewish sources, and the essence of all Torah can be put into three words!" He pulled out a small, worn-out notebook from his jacket pocket, and put on his glasses. Flipping through the book, he finally found what he was searching for. Looking up, he said, "Measure for measure." *Midah c'neged midah.* That was it.

I sat in wonder. Here I was in a synagogue in the middle of India. Had this rabbi ever learned any Indian philosophy? Did he know that what he just told me was also one of the primary principles behind Eastern spirituality? Was there a clearer way of stating the Law of Karma, the Hindu concept that whatever you do affects everything in your life and in everyone else's life, in this lifetime and the next? Measure for measure.

Judaism says that God measures everything out to us. What we receive depends on our need and on our ability to learn from it. As the Mishna says, "To love God ... with all your might (*m'o'decha*)," means that "for every single measure (*midah*) that God measures out to you, give thanks (*modeh*) to God very (*m'od*), very much." Ultimately, everything is from God, and we have to struggle with it and cope with it and give thanks for it, whatever it may be.

21

SWAMI HARIHARANANDA: It Takes More Than a Man-tra to Become a Man

Not far from Calcutta, I stayed in the homes of two devotees of Paramahansa Yogananda, and while there I read his book, *Autobiography of a Yogi*, which made a deep impression on me. Yogananda's teacher was Swami Yogashwar, whose ashram was in Puri, just south of Calcutta. I visited this large, beautiful place and was shown around by Swami Hariharananda, who was now the master in this lineage. I had heard very amazing stories about him. He was a master of kriya yoga. In kriya yoga, mastery of breath is mastery of self. Through a practice of the breath, and a love of the breath, we can be totally connected to God.

While the swami was showing me around the ashram, I commented on how peaceful it felt and what it must have been like at the time of Swami Yogashwar.

"When Swami Yogashwar was in charge, it was not so peaceful and still," he said. "The silence was always broken by people crying from the difficult *sadhana*, the deep inner spiritual work they were struggling with." He said that now it was much different.

When I asked if he would initiate me into kriya yoga, he turned me down. "A rolling stone gathers no moss." He said. "Roaming is contrary to finding inner peace. Come back in a year when you're ready to really sit and pursue the practice. These days, everyone thinks you just need to chant a mantra over and over again and you'll become a holy person. Can you practice medicine because you have a medical book, or because you chant 'doctor, doctor, doctor' all day, or because you give flowers to the pictures of great doctors? No. You need a teacher and seclusion to learn properly. Similarly with kriya yoga. It's long and arduous work and there is no getting around it."

I was disappointed and a little wounded. I was used to everyone being so happy to meet me and take me into their teachings. This was a real challenge to my wandering way, a powerful statement and an important warning. There are no shortcuts, and even enlightenment rarely removes the necessity of doing the deep inner work on your self.

22

SAI BABA:
Getting Enough to Eat

Usually, I received special treatment almost everywhere I went. This was primarily due to coming in the name of my teacher, Sri Pad, and because it was very unusual for a Westerner to be a sadhu. Though I loved it, this honor was really very embarrassing because I knew that I wasn't so holy and that I had just begun this path. Nonetheless, I was getting used to being taken care of. This was true in private homes and ashrams where Sri Pad sent me. In some of these homes, I began hearing stories of a guru I had not heard of before. People told of his mystical visits in the middle of the night and how indentations of his footprints were left in their cement floor.

I knew I had to visit the ashram of this guru, Sri Satya Sai Baba. It was in central India, near Bangalore, and when I got there I realized that it was very different from what I was accustomed to in a number of ways. This was a guru-centered community. Though he taught that we should love everyone and serve everyone—and it was truly practiced to perfection—still the greatest love and devotion and service seemed to revolve around him. It was quite understandable. Sai Baba was widely known for performing miracles—healing, traveling beyond the limits of space and time, and materializing objects. Everyone at the ashram seemed to have a story about miracles he had done for them. For example, there were many stories of someone asking for a certain kind of camera or watch. Sai Baba would pause for a minute or two, or perhaps go behind a curtain, and return with the camera or watch or whatever with the purchase slip from a specialty store, perhaps in New York City. When the person went to New York City, he would go to the store, and a clerk would recall that an unusual-looking black man with a big afro and wearing a long, ankle-length, bright orange shirt had come in, on that specific date, asked for that particular item, paid with exact change, walked out, and disappeared.

Sai Baba dressed in electric saffron-orange cloth. He had a very striking appearance. His features, in contrast to most Indians, were very African, with a broad nose and a wide, thick, black afro-halo standing straight out from his head. He struck quite an imposing appearance in his saffron robe. But more than his appearance was an aura created by his graceful, powerful, loving presence as he walked through the crowds that had come to see him. Some were there because he had healed or helped them; others were there seeking help or healing.

This was such a contrast to the teachers I had been with. With them, no one wore orange, there was no outward display of miracles (though many happened), and there were no crowds. But to top it all off, I was shocked that Sai Baba didn't provide for sadhus! He felt everyone should contribute to his community through some kind of work—cleaning, gardening, cooking, or applying his or her professional skills as a doctor, for instance. The kitchen made large quantities of food several times a day, but you had to work for it or pay for it. I had nothing against work, not after two years on a kibbutz. But at that time in my development as a sadhu, I was determined to stay outside the societal norms and structures. I felt that doing this would strengthen my faith. (This is similar to the debate in Israel over yeshiva students "just" sitting and learning as their contribution to the broader society.) So living very simply on a diet of tea, bananas, yogurt, and peanuts, I learned to make the little bit of money I had last as long as possible.

Each day began with an early morning meditation, followed by Sai Baba making a brief appearance, called *darshan*, on his balcony. Then his disciples would come down the rows of us who had been meditating. They carried trays of tea biscuits, and each person got one or two. These were called *prasad*, a little gift from the guru (similar to the *shiriiem* that a rebbe or *tzaddik* would eat from, before handing out the rest to his followers). *Prasad* was intended as nourishment for the Soul, not for the body. But I couldn't help appreciating it both ways; after all, for the sadhu, everything that came our way was a gift from God.

One particular morning, instead of regular, rectangular biscuits, the *prasad* was tiny and round, smaller than a dime. A devotee bent down and gave a small handful of these biscuits to each of us. I was sure that I wouldn't get enough to eat from that.

As the man bent down in front of me, he lost his balance, and the whole tray poured into my lap. This wasn't the sort of thing that you can give back. "Whatever measure God measures out for you, be very, very grateful." As I scooped all the biscuits into my pockets, I knew this was going to be a very, very interesting day.

No sooner was I on my feet and walking away when a woman came up to me and said, "Here's ten rupees. Make sure you get enough to eat today." I looked at the ten rupee bill and thought, "Wow, this is great! This can last a long time."

I headed to my usual tea shop and asked for my regular meal of tea, banana, yogurt, and peanuts. I was going to splurge and eat them all at once, instead of stretching it out over the whole day. When my food came, the man at the next table insisted on paying for the meal, saying that it was an honor to help a sadhu from the West.

Again in the late afternoon someone paid for my food. Later, as I walked past the ashram kitchen, which had just finished serving the evening meal, the man in charge motioned for me to come over. I thought he needed a hand lifting a large pot. I came over to him and he handed me a full plate of food, saying, "Here's something for you. You never get enough to eat! Take this and enjoy." You have to understand: they *never* gave out free food!

As I just finished that extremely generous measure, a car pulled up and some Americans who were staying at the ashram got out. One of the women said, "We were just in Bangalore, shopping, and we got all sorts of treats. We brought some food for you, too. You never get enough to eat." And they handed me more food.

I hadn't been so stuffed in ages. I went to the tree in the field where I usually slept. I woke up several times from an upset stomach. Somehow I knew that God, and Sri Pad, and Sai Baba, were all laughing, and saying, "So, you don't think you'll get enough to eat?"

23

SAI BABA: "I'm Sorry. I Made a Mistake. Please Forgive Me."

Most of my experiences in India led to new breakthroughs and insights, and there was no question in my mind or heart that they were happening through the consciousness, awareness, and love of these enlightened teachers who were guiding me from near and far. Thus, I attribute these experiences in Sai Baba's backyard to him. Ultimately, I was learning again and again that everything is from God, who interacts with each of us, exactly where we are.

The dress code at Sai Baba's ashram required that we wear white and that women dress modestly, including covering their arms. Among the people at the ashram was an American named Jenny. She was a wonderful spiritual balladeer and songwriter—and quite a character. Her arms were uncovered.

One of the ashram supervisors approached her and very gently asked her to please cover her arms. Jenny politely said no. The man said to her quite nicely, "You'd make a lot of people happy if you would cover your arms."

"People's happiness shouldn't depend on whether my arms are covered or not!" she said with strength, conviction, and a little defiance.

"Then I'm afraid we'll have to ask you to leave."

At this point, I innocently intervened, trying to make peace. I suggested that maybe it wasn't so bad, and after all it was very hot, and there must be some kind of resolution to this problem.

"And you should leave as well!" the supervisor said to me.

Me? I didn't do anything wrong; I was just trying to help. How could he ask me to leave? Before I knew it, as if materialized out of nowhere, six ashram "ushers" forcefully carried me to the entrance. I struggled with them, shouting, "Where is the love that Baba teaches about?" I felt like I was in an old Western movie, being thrown out of the saloon. I picked myself off the ground and brushed off the dust, quite shaken by what had happened.

What could I do? How could this be? Just then an American woman came over, pointing out that my sleeve had been torn. "What happened?" she asked. I told her what I *thought* happened. She said, "Well, didn't you complain the other day that you were too hot having to wear a shirt here? It looks like Baba has ventilated your shirt." I wasn't quite ready for that explanation. Eager to resolve the situation, she said, "I'm sure there's been some mistake. But don't worry. We'll go to the person in charge and everything will be okay."

"But, he's the one who asked me to leave."

"Oh dear! Well, never mind, we'll just go and talk to him. Just listen to what I say, and repeat it after me, okay?"

We went over to the man who had just thrown me out and exchanged a few words. Then she said, "I'm sorry. I made a mistake. Please forgive me." She signaled that that was my cue to repeat after her.

(I thought to myself, "What? *I'm* not sorry, and *I* didn't make a mistake, so what do *I* need his forgiveness for!")

She waited patiently for me to deliver my lines. Speaking through clenched teeth, and looking anywhere but in his eyes, I mumbled, "I'm sorry. I made a mistake. Please forgive me." Talk about insincerity.

Looking me right in the eye, he said, "I'm sorry. *I* made a mistake. Please forgive *me*." He said it with full sincerity, from the heart.

I felt a little nauseous from my own insincerity, or perhaps from eating such a large slice of humble pie.

And that was it! I was back in the ashram's good graces. It was all okay.

I was so blown away from that experience, from the simplicity of asking for forgiveness, that I began trying it out as a kind of mantra. As I passed a tree, I'd realize that I passed it all the time but never really stopped to look at it, to see it, to acknowledge its existence, its beauty, and its Godly essence. So I'd say to the tree, "I'm sorry. I made a mistake. Please forgive me." And so on, with people and things; I was asking forgiveness from the whole world and from the Creator. How could I ever be so sure that I didn't make a mistake? So sure, that I wasn't at all sorry? So sure, that I didn't need to ask anyone for forgiveness?

As I strolled around, I remembered a teaching of Rabbi Nachman of Breslov that I had learned from Shlomo Carlebach. Shlomo would say, "What right do I have to step on the stones or the grass? Without acknowledging that God creates everything, gives life to everything, and is the sustaining life force in everything—what right do I have to make use of anything in this world?"

This lesson from Shlomo and from the incident at Sai Baba's ashram both encapsulated the steps in the Jewish concept of *teshuvah:* repenting, being aware of what you've done, feeling regret, asking forgiveness, resolving not to do it again, and putting yourself in a similar situation and refraining from repeating the same mistake. To all these approaches, Hindu and Jewish, the basics: I'm sorry. I made a mistake. Please forgive me.

24

SAI BABA:
Healing and Charity

One day, I was at the tea shop just down the road from Sai Baba's ashram where I always ate. An Indian man, with a young boy of six or seven at his side, said, "Swamiji!" ("Ji" adds a dimension of endearment to the formal title of swami.) I looked around to see who he was speaking to. Nobody else was there. I realized he was talking to me. "Swamiji, please heal my son!"

I began to put together the pieces of this puzzling exchange. We were a few minutes from Sai Baba's ashram. People came here from all over India for miracles, for healing, for help, for inspiration. In fact, they came from all over the world. If he was asking me to heal his son, it was pretty clear that he had come here hoping that Sai Baba would heal him. Apparently, that hadn't happened. Now he was going to try any other holy man who was around. And here I was. Remember, to most Indians, someone from the West who has given up the wealth of our culture is very holy and held in high regard.

I looked at his son—a beautiful, happy boy, with shining, dark round eyes. He didn't look sick to me. I smiled at him, looked him in the eyes, and he flashed a warm smile back to me.

I explained to the father that I was neither a swami nor a healer. But I asked how I could help. He said that his son was deaf, and he wanted him to be healed.

I took a deep breath and prayed for wisdom and guidance. "You went to Sai Baba?" I asked the father.

"Yes, but he didn't heal him."

"Maybe he did heal him." I said. "Sometimes it takes days or months or even years for the healing to come through. Perhaps you should have more faith in the process, and give it more time."

I continued: "Your son seems so bright, healthy, and lively. He seems to be doing quite well. Maybe his deafness is a gift from God, to teach you to listen and speak from your heart."

He answered, "But I want my son to be perfect."

"All God's children are perfect. Our job is to try to understand God's perfection." I don't know where these words came from. They just flowed through me.

We spoke for a while longer. I blessed them for healing and wholeness, and understanding and patience, and that God should make their lives as full and as meaningful as they could possibly dream. Soon, we parted and went our separate ways. I was moved by our encounter, and humbled also, knowing that the wisdom I had offered the father and son really wasn't from me.

A few weeks later, my travels brought me to an American Express office where I could pick up my mail. A letter was waiting from my sister. She wanted me to know that her youngest son had been diagnosed as deaf. I was so sorry for him and for her. I felt such pity. And then I caught myself. I needed to hear the words I had spoken to that desperate father and his son. I was amazed at the synchronicity of these events—first that Indian father and his son, now my sister and her son.

I sat down and wrote my sister that just a short time ago someone had asked me to heal his deaf son. If I had known my nephew was deaf, I told her, and someone had said those words to me, I wasn't sure whether I could have *heard* him. Yet, I felt that this understanding and insight had come to me from God and that I had to share it with her. It was still up to all of us to somehow accept this new reality and see her son as a gift from God, as another of His perfect children, and to give thanks to God, very, very much.

Sai Baba could have taken me aside and told me that my nephew was deaf, but I don't think it would have been as effective as *learning* about it the way I did. I have to assume the same was true for the father of the deaf boy.

Sometimes, between the group meditations and chanting, and Sai Baba's appearances, I would go for meditative walks. No destination, just a slow easy pace, letting my thoughts slow down and disappear. Becoming more and more *present* in the moment, I could feel God's *Presence* more and more. It is always there, but the veils come down endlessly and require constant attention to draw them back, again and again.

As I walked down the road, a beggar boy held out his hand and said, "Bakshish?" The gesture and the word were clearly asking for charity.

Again, here I was the sadhu, who had nothing; and the Westerner, who must have something. And around the ashram, there were lots of Westerners who probably gave charity to the beggars.

I pointed to myself and my attire (barefoot and a simple cloth wrapped around me) and said, "Sadhu," meaning, "Hey, I'm a sadhu, I don't have money to give."

He looked at me in consternation, pointed to me and said, "Poor?" (Somehow, he spoke this in English.)

I nodded in the affirmative, lifting my hands toward the heavens, and said, "Poor."

He looked at me, trying to resolve the dissonance between sadhu and Westerner. Then he reached into his begging cup, took out a coin, and offered it to me!

Once again, I was overwhelmed by this awakening slap from the Universe, from God, and from all His teacher-helpers. This young boy, poor and destitute, had the compassion and the generosity to give to someone he thought had even less than he. Or maybe he was compassionate because he knew I had more than he did. Maybe he felt sorry for me because although I had chosen a lifestyle of simplicity, I still felt it as lacking—even as a sadhu! I may have been quite *present*, but I wasn't ready to give *presents*. And so God's *Presence* couldn't really dwell here. This beggar helped wake me up again.

I stopped and shouted joyously, "No, I'm not poor! You're only poor if you always want things! I'm not poor! I'm free!" I gave him his money back, plus a little extra, then I sat down and wrote this song:

You're only poor by the measure of desire,
Beggars—for the love of God!
Thirsty fish. Thirsty fish.
It's ignorance that makes you dry, makes you high,
  and makes you die,
Slaves in timeless chains,
Now is the key to the lock of illusion.

Calling his followers "Holy Beggars," Shlomo Carlebach would say, "My Holy Beggars aren't begging for you to give them something. They're begging, 'Please, is there something I can do for you?' 'HaShem! Please! Is there something I can do for You?' *That's* a Holy Beggar." "You know why it's so hard to give *tzadakah*, charity?" he once asked. "Because you think the money is yours!"

When you stop thinking about yourself and start thinking about others, you can enter the now, and you can be free in the present.

25

SAI BABA:
My Private Interview

Almost every day, Sai Baba would come out from his private quarters and walk through the crowds of people who had gathered to see him, waiting for blessings or healing. Many hoped that he would point to them, indicating that they were chosen to have a private session with him. In these "interviews," he would talk briefly to a group, then would take each person aside and talk to him privately behind a curtain, revealing things going on in his life or in his personal thoughts and offering advice. Usually, he would return to the whole group to heal someone or materialize different things for certain people.

I also hoped to meet with Sai Baba. I wasn't sick or needy, and he wasn't my guru with whom I badly wanted a private *darshan*. It was more that I felt like I was sent here, or called here. Sri Pad and others had told me to come here, and I felt that a greater lesson was entwined in all this than just coming to Sai Baba's ashram and seeing him at a distance. Of course, I was on my spiritual quest, and was always looking for more help and blessings on my journey to God. In fact, sometimes I felt like I needed a good kick in the pants to keep me on that path. Finally, one day, while waiting with everyone else, Sai Baba passed by, pointed to me, and I went inside his interview room.

All of us who had been chosen were led into a small room with a curtained area. When it was my turn, Sai Baba took me behind the curtain so we could speak privately. He spoke quite quickly about a number of things, including my waking up in the middle of the night with an upset stomach ("Getting enough to eat?"). He talked about my meditation practice. Commenting on my difficulty concentrating for long periods, he advised that I say a simple mantra, such as "Om," twice a day. He also said he would give me prayer beads to help me focus. Then he waved his hand, palm down, in a circular motion, and a string of glass meditation beads, a *mala*, appeared to materialize out of his hand. He gave me the beads and said a few words about hanging the beads over my index finger and counting them, pulling them between my thumb and my other fingers. This, he said, would symbolize ego, soul, and the Divine.

I gained tremendous insight about being cared for and caring for others while in Sai Baba's "sphere of influence." Over the years, I have met a number of people through my connection to Sai Baba. I continue to value my experiences with him, and these stories are among my favorites. I left his ashram deeply grateful for the opportunity to have had a close encounter with him. At the same time, I was also very grateful that my relationships with Reb Shlomo and Sri Pad were much more personal. After being with Sai Baba, I was much more aware that the miracles are there all the time.

26

THE MOTHER:
"Three Percent Is Better
Than Everything"

I left Sai Baba's ashram and continued the journey that Sri
Pad had sent me on. I had started to read some of Sri
Aurobindo's elegant philosophical spiritual writings while I
was still at Baba's. I liked his way of articulating a person's
spiritual evolution and admired his intellectual acuity. So I set
off for the Sri Aurobindo Ashram, ready for a new adventure.

"Mother" is a title of spiritual achievement for women in
India. The Mother of the ashram worked in partnership with
Sri Aurobindo for fifty years, and after his passing, she became
the spiritual leader of both the ashram and its experimental
utopian village, Auroville. Sri Aurobindo, her mentor and partner, was very unusual. Educated in England, he spoke English
fluently and eloquently. He became very active in opposing the
British occupation of India, and while serving a lengthy jail
sentence, he had an enlightenment experience and shifted his
role from activist to guru. Unlike other spiritual teachers in
India, his teachings were written originally in English. It was
said that while Gandhi was a guru in politician's garb, Sri
Aurobindo was a politician in guru's clothing. Sri Aurobindo
spoke about the "Supramental Consciousness" of the evolved
individual and the evolved society. I had heard about Auroville
when researching kibbutzim, communes, and intentional communities. Its approach to spiritual awakening and develop-

ment was wrapped around the sense of a conscious and intentional community, not around worshipping a guru.

At the Sri Aurobindo Ashram, the Mother was not being worshipped, as far as I could see. Nor were the other influential teachers along my path. I have a wonderful respect for her and this is a story I made up from what I learned from her:

Someone prostrated before the Mother, saying, "Mother, I had a dream about you a few years ago. I didn't even know who you were. Then several months ago, I was at a friend's house. On his meditation table, among other pictures, was a picture of you. I asked, 'Who is this? I had a dream about her over a year ago!' I was so excited. I asked him all about you and where you were. I knew you were meant to be my guru. I returned home and began making plans to come to you. I sold all my possessions, gave up my apartment, booked my flight, and here I am." Prostrating before her again, he said, "Mother, I surrender myself to you. Please accept me as your devotee."

The Mother smiled at him, bowed slightly, and said, "Thank you. I accept your three percent."

"Three percent?" he said, peeling himself off the floor. "But I just surrendered myself to you completely!"

Very kindly, she responded, "Let's be honest here. How much of yourself do you have control over to surrender to me? Listen, three percent isn't bad. It beats the national average. So I graciously accept your three percent. Now go and work on yourself some more, and when you have more to offer, I will happily accept, a little at a time."

Many gurus would have said, "Thank you. I accept your total surrender. Now go and bring me ninety-seven more followers." They would rather keep you thinking you're totally conscious, while keeping you 97 percent unconscious—the better to manipulate you. The Mother would have none of that. She wanted you to work for your own realization.

I have been telling this story for more than thirty years, trying to warn people of the dynamics of the spiritual games some gurus can play.

In the early 1970s, I was leading workshops at annual conferences of the Association of Humanistic Psychology and the Association of Transpersonal Psychology when a presenter at one of these conferences suggested that all the meditation and spirituality teachers meet to share our common interests. We gathered in a fairly small room. It quickly filled up, and after an opening meditation, someone suggested that we go around the room and introduce ourselves.

"Hello, my name is so-and-so. I'm a disciple of the enlightened master so-and-so."

"I am so-and-so. I'm a devotee of the realized master so-and-so."

"My name is so-and-so. I'm the follower of the transcended master.... "

"Hello, my name is so-and-so. I'm a teacher of the reincarnated master so-and-so."

"So-and-so is my name. I'm a disciple of the perfected master so-and-so."

I think you get the idea. When it was finally my turn (somehow, I was the last), I said, "Shalom. My name is David and I come from a long line of unperfected and unenlightened masters. We've been making mistakes and missing God's message for more than four thousand years. But we're getting it together. We're getting there.... "

There was a laugh of relief. I had helped put everything into a more human, lovable framework.

So the Mother was very important in putting the process of surrender into perspective. Surrendering your self and your possessions to the guru has many stages, many levels, and many ways of application. The Mother taught that whatever you had, or needed, or even whatever you were feeling—good or bad, happy or sad—you should offer it up to the guru, or to God. Our strong attachments to our feelings and possessions give them a life and strength that they would not have otherwise. By offering up our emotions or our material obsessions, they take on a higher form. From our love of ice cream, we can learn about the dynamics of love. And we can elevate that love of ice cream to a love of humanity and eventually, of God. We can go from a personal obsession to an obligation to other persons.

Sleeping outside on someone's roof near the Sri Aurobindo Ashram, I woke up early one morning on the wrong side of the bed. Well, I didn't actually have a bed; I guess I woke up on the wrong side of the roof. To be more accurate, I woke up on the "wrong" side of the world.

Living in the moment as a sadhu in India was very different from living in the West. It required a totally different mindset because the West is so focused on achieving, accumulating, and being aggressive: Be someone! No time to *live*—got to make a *living*. Make a *killing* on the market.

This particular morning, I woke up in the "Western hemisphere," the left hemisphere of my brain. It was one of those mornings of reflecting on what I was doing with my life: Where was I going? What was I accomplishing? How was I going to get a job after living like a sadhu? How would I contribute to society? I guess you could call it waking up in my parental, cultural standards and expectations. Even my Jungian, archetypal parents must have had a lot of trouble with my going to such lengths in my "process of individuation," in my finding my true Self in my own unique way. Individuate, okay, but do it the way *we* do it!

I had been out of the U.S. for much of the past several years, yet, somehow during the night, I had slipped out of the here and now and fallen into the "there and then." I was ready for the blues. This showed promise of being a major bummer until I remembered the Mother's teaching: "Give it to me. Give it to God. Don't hold on to the good or the bad. Don't indulge yourself."

I sat up, meditated, and shouted in silence, "Mother! You can have this! I don't want it! Take it away!"

Within moments, the gloom left. Free, I was back in my right brain, my Eastern hemisphere, back in the here and now. And I could see from that perspective what I was doing with my life and where I was going: getting closer to God and to my soul's true purpose in life. I knew my accomplishments were beyond measure and judgment. They were not in the material world but in the psychological and spiritual world. I knew I had accumulated a wealth of knowledge and experience of God.

Of course, I didn't know that one day I would make a living giving spiritual teachings or even writing a book about my spiritual encounters. But I did see that I was in God's hands and He was taking care of me. All I needed to do was learn to stay in the moment, now and in the future, and all would be well.

27

THE MOTHER: "Sh'ma Yisrael"

When Sri Pad had told me to go to the Sri Aurobindo Ashram, he had also given me the name of Sister Diana, a Frenchwoman who had helped him when he had come here many years before. She arranged for me to have *darshan* with the Mother, who was ninety-four. *Darshan* with the Mother was very rare; even people living at the ashram got to see her only once a year, usually on their birthday.

The procedure for a *darshan* was first to meditate at the grave of Sri Aurobindo. Then someone would tap you on the shoulder as a way to tell you it was time to go upstairs to the *darshan* room. You were given flowers and waited in line until your turn. To show your respect, you presented the flowers to the Mother, made eye contact with her as long as possible, then respectfully took your leave.

While meditating before seeing her, I began reciting a mantra practiced at the ashram. Suddenly, I felt an electric-like surge. There was a flash of white light and I saw and heard the essential Jewish mantra of God's Unity: *"Sh'ma Yisrael, HaShem Elokaynu, HaShem Echad,"* "Hear, O Israel, The Lord Is Our God, The Lord Is One." This coincided with multiple levels of understanding and revelations of depth and meaning—not intellectually, but experientially—and not in the head, but in the heart.

I experienced the words "Hear, O Israel" as a call to listen from the depths of my being and soul. I was shown that

Judaism doesn't say the Four-Lettered Name "Lord" (YHVH) as it is spelled and could be pronounced in Hebrew because we're meant to experience God each time we see and say the Name of God.

Language puts labels on all kinds of experiences so that instead of really seeing and hearing a waterfall energetically and experientially, each growing child learns to recognize the picture-book image of the real object, and then to identify with its name and label.

I was *experiencing* that God's Oneness wasn't about being the only God or the One monotheistic God. God's One was the *All-Inclusive* One, the One that includes everything and everyone in all of existence. I was blown away, and for a moment, I was in Eternity. I felt and knew that I was a part of the Whole. I was One with God. I was home again.

Just then, someone tapped me on the shoulder. It was my turn to see the Mother. I was already quite beyond myself. I went up the stairs and waited in line, watching others bow, present their flowers, and engage in eye contact. The Mother looked very old and fragile. I figured I should be able to maintain good eye contact. My turn came, and when I looked into her eyes, Eternity stared back at me. It was a deep and penetrating gaze, full of presence and power. It wasn't so easy to meet it and hold it. On the other hand, I was still filled with my earlier experience of the *Sh'ma*.

Afterward, Sister Diana asked me how my *darshan* was.

"It was very moving," I said, "but I had an even more powerful experience right before going up to see her—a very profound Jewish experience."

"Well," she answered, very matter-of-factly, "you know, the Mother was Jewish."

Well, I didn't know that. Only then did I learn she had come from a French-Jewish family that had come to the French colony of Pondicherry in India for a vacation in 1914. She met Sri Aurobindo, they felt a very strong bond, and she returned to be his spiritual partner.

The symbol of the ashram was two triangles intersecting, one pointing up, and one pointing down, forming a six-pointed star. In the center was a square, and in that was a lotus. To me, this was clearly the Magen David, the Jewish star, with a lotus, the symbol of meditation, in the center. It was my symbol of how to blend East and West, Jewish and Indian. I bought a small lead charm, put it on my prayer beads, and began chanting *Sh'ma Yisrael* as my mantra, filled with all the meaning that had been revealed to me.

I still wear that star with the lotus around my neck, and the mantra has become an integral part of my traditional Jewish prayers and meditation practice.

28

COCHIN: "Jew Town!"

The rabbi in Calcutta must have thought I had become a sadhu out of poverty, because he told me that if I needed any kind of help—financial or otherwise—I should visit Mr. Kodah, who lived in the Jewish community of Cochin. He told me just ask for Mr. Kodah, that everyone knew him. That wasn't on the itinerary that Sri Pad had outlined for me, but I felt compelled to use this opportunity to meet the Jews of Cochin.

I arrived in Cochin by train. At the bus station, I was told to take a certain bus to get to Mr. Kodah. When the bus arrived, I told the driver I was going to see Mr. Kodah. Take a seat, he said, and he'd call me when it was my stop.

We drove on for some time. Finally the driver called out, "Jew Town!" I was horrified. Was this a ghetto? Was Chochin full of anti-Semites? The driver smiled at me, wagging his head in that Indian way, motioning that this was my stop. Was I being deported? Was this a friendly one-way trip to who-knew-where?

I got off the bus. A sign indicated that the street was, indeed, named "Jew Town." Hesitantly, I asked someone where I could find Mr. Kodah. He pointed down the street, and I walked in that direction. There were no guards, no police, no army—nothing that suggested this was a ghetto. People seemed happy. They walked about freely. They didn't seem suppressed or intimidated.

I found Mr. Kodah's house and introduced myself as a Jew from America and Israel. I was warmly received. Mr. Kodah and his family fed me generously and promised to show me around the next day. They gave me a room with a bed to sleep in. It had been many months since I had had a bedroom, let alone been in a bed. My first night indoors, I was wakened by something fuzzy, fluttering, and scratching in my beard. I jumped up and brushed it away. It was a bat! And I thought I had to be careful when I slept outside!

Other than that, the Kodahs' hospitality was wonderful. The next day, they showed me around. I learned that Chochin was the oldest Jewish community in the world, outside of Israel, and the only Jewish community that had lived in peace, undisturbed by any anti-Semitism, for nearly two thousand years, since, in fact, Jews had come here after the destruction of the Holy Temple in Jerusalem. It was called "Jew Town" because Jews lived here. That's all. It was no slur, no defamation.

The Kodahs took me to their synagogue. The oldest and longest-standing synagogue in the world, it had stood unattacked, unburned, undestroyed for two millennia. For almost all that time, their community had remained intact, with a strong Jewish identity. It took the creation of the State of Israel in 1948 to almost totally remove the vast majority of Jews from Chochin. Within a short time, they had immigrated to Israel.

The Kodahs' love of Jews and of Israel was so beautiful, and their hospitality was warm and welcoming. I felt like the wandering Hasid who is told that in such-and-such a town, a wealthy man opens his house to all. If your horse is worn out, he gives you a new one and sends you on your way with new energy and direction and conviction, reminding you, once again, that it is really God who is taking care of you.

After my experience of the Sh'ma at the Sri Aurobindo Ashram, I knew I was on my way back to Judaism. Little did I know that I was also on my way back to Israel.

29

Farewell to Sri Pad and India

After six months of making a pilgrimage around India, I returned to Vrindavan and to Sri Pad. It was wonderful to be "home" again, yet I knew I wasn't *home*. The power of my Jewish meditation experience at the Sri Aurobindo Ashram had made it clear that my home was in Judaism and in the West.

The opportunities for spiritual advancement with Sri Pad were still very real and tangible and important to me. He had made it clear to me at the beginning that he wasn't assuming that I was staying in India or becoming a Hindu. He had even said that it didn't matter.

Sri Pad offered me the chance to study classical Indian flute with a master musician. Music would become my spiritual practice and meditation. If I would submerge myself in it, if I would surrender to it, I could become a master musician myself. That wasn't a guarantee, but it was a sure potential. In this framework of spiritual devotion through music, you are not studying to perform for the public. You are perfecting yourself and your instrument for the sole purpose—and the Soul Purpose—of playing for God alone. By surrendering, you become God's instrument. God plays through you. Inspiring me was a classic Indian story of a musician who was considered the greatest sitar player—though no one had ever heard him play. He only played in the middle of the night in a vast garden that was closed to the public. And there he played for God. Here's the tale:

A great raja, an Indian king, heard about him and sent messengers inviting him to play for the king in the palace.

To the king's astonishment, the musician turned down the invitation, explaining, "I only play for God."

The king sent out messengers a second time, telling them to make it clear that aside from the honor of playing for the king, he would also be rewarded with great wealth. Again he refused. "I only play music for the King of Kings."

The king was more curious than mad. What kind of person would turn down honor and wealth? And what rhapsodic kind of music does he play? So he disguised himself as a commoner and traveled to the village where the musician lived. The king went into the garden during the day, and hid in the bushes before they locked it up for the night.

Just before midnight, the musician came, settled down and took out his sitar. First he meditated, attuning himself to God, and then he picked up the sitar and began tuning it. This was done with such presence, devotion, and love that just the sounds of tuning were too much for the raja. He was so deeply moved that he briefly fainted, letting out a sigh as he swooned.

The musician heard the sound, and called out, "Who's there? Come out this minute and reveal yourself!"

The king came out, apologizing profusely and falling at the feet of the musician. "Please forgive me," he begged. "I just had to hear what your music sounded like. But know that I am a great and wealthy king, and you will not go away unrewarded."

"I need no reward," the musician said. "Please depart from this garden and leave me alone."

"Please," the king pleaded, "there must be something I can do for you."

"All right," the musician said impatiently, "fill the crack in that step over there."

"No, you don't understand. I can do great things. Why do you ask me to do such an unworthy task?"

"You don't see, do you?" said the musician. And he reached over and touched him on the forehead.

Suddenly, the king saw that the musician, in his selfless devotion, dwelt in an entirely different realm of consciousness. Now he saw that the stone step was, in fact, encrusted with the most precious gems. He realized that his entire wealth was not enough to fill the tiny crack in the step. He discovered his true place and value in God's kingdom. He returned home a very different, and a very humble, man.

The opportunity to learn Indian flute was very enticing. But my heart wasn't in it. My visa was about to expire and I had to apply for an extension. I turned the decision of staying over to God. Either I get the visa extension—or I don't.

I went to the government office. An official asked, "Why do you want to extend your visa?"

"My teacher wants me to stay and study classical flute."

(But to myself, I said, "Please say no. I'm really ready to go home.")

He told me to wait outside. Shortly, I was called back in. My request had been granted. Now what would I do?

Back in Vrindavan, I realized this was not just in God's hands. It was in *my* hands. I couldn't passively let someone make this decision for me—not even God! I told Sri Pad that it was really time for me to return to America to integrate my incredible experiences in Israel and India with my life in the West.

He completely accepted my decision and gave me his blessings. He told me to bathe one more time in the holy Yamuna River and to get my long hair cut. He also told me to buy a pair of pants and some simple rubber thongs, because I couldn't go on a plane barefoot.

As I packed my few possessions, I kept glancing at a watercolor painting that one of Sri Pad's followers had painted. I wanted it for a keepsake. I packed everything, leaving the painting out, then returned to where Sri Pad and his entourage were sitting. I sort of backed into the room, shyly saying, "I cannot steal!"

To my chagrin, they started laughing. When I had left to gather my things, Sri Pad had said, "If he steals the picture, he can have it. But if he asks for it, then he can't have it." They laughed so hard. How had Sri Pad known I wanted to take it? And how did he know my conflict over taking it? As with the visa, I had to learn to make my own choices and live with the consequences.

It was a wonderful send-off, very human and just right and light. Not too heavy or profound. This was not a time to take myself too seriously. It was time to return home a very different person than when I had left, years before: a more humble person, a more Jewish person, a more sensitive person.

30

The Sadhu Comes Home

Getting clothes and a haircut and saying good-bye to everyone in India was one thing. Coming back to America was something else. My hair was still long by conventional standards, and my clothes were Indian. At customs in Los Angeles, they took one look at me and went through all of my very few possessions with a fine-tooth comb. I had quite a collection of interesting UFOs—unidentifiable foreign objects: little packets of ash, *vebuti,* and the glass prayer beads Sai Baba had materialized; wooden prayer beads; a hardened ball of clay from the holy ground of Vrindavan; pressed flowers and various other gifts from Sri Pad; and dried leaves from the banyan tree that Buddha had sat under when he became enlightened. I also had my bamboo flute and the original silver flute I had brought with me to India.

The customs official opened everything, sniffed everything, and tasted every ash and every powder.

Condescendingly, calling me by my first name, he asked about each thing, "What's this, *Dave?*"

I answered as nonchalantly as I could.

"That's ash that a swami materialized."

"That's earth from a very holy village."

"Those are flowers from a special ceremony."

Unwrapping a piece of paper, to his delight and my total surprise, he found a very tiny amount of marijuana.

"Well, *Dave,* what have we here?"

You have to understand: the whole time I was in India (and quite a long time before that), I never smoked anything. Not on *my* spiritual journey. "A swami gave that to me for protection." I told him, "I didn't even know what was in it until you opened it."

"Gee, *Dave,* this isn't even enough to get high on."

I figured I didn't have anything to lose, so I said, "Well, when you meditate a lot, it really doesn't take very much to get you high."

He did a double take, checking me out one more time. Then he handed me my things and said, "Go on! Get out of here."

Being back home was really wonderful, but it was not an easy transition. I wasn't sure I wanted to give up my asceticism and my simple life so quickly. In fact, the first few nights home, I slept on the ground in the backyard, wrapped in a blanket, as I'd done in India.

I bathed in cold water, pouring the water over myself, soaping and rinsing, just as I had done in India. I washed my few clothes by hand in the bathtub. My parents were a bit nervous, but they patiently gave me space to return slowly to Southern California without getting the "bends" from coming up too quickly through the culture shock.

31

INTRA-REALITIES: Awakening and Transition—Integrating East and West

While still in India, I had written to Roger Bell, who had been the dean of men at Pomona College. He was now a dean at the University of Redlands in Southern California. We had become good friends through my work at Pomona, particularly through the conference on "The Experience of Self-Discovery" that I had organized in 1968. In my letter to him, I had tried to explain what I was experiencing in India. Wherever I was "at" when I coordinated the conference, I told him, he could multiply it by a million to begin to appreciate where I was now. I told him I had no idea what God had in mind for me once I came back to the West, and I asked whether there was any work that he could find that would be fitting for me. He wrote back that he couldn't get me a faculty position but he could find me a job on campus, and that once I was there he was sure I would make my own way.

He got me a position as residential director of a dormitory at the university. Primarily, I supervised the undergraduates living in the dorm. The job left a lot of free time, so I could pursue other possibilities on campus.

I was provided with a spacious apartment attached to the dorm, with a living room, bedroom, kitchen, and bathroom. To me, this was like a palace. I walked in, carrying a cardboard box of my belongings, and scanned the large space. Roger asked whether he could help carry in my other things from the car, and I explained that this was all I had.

Just a few years earlier, the university had started an experimental college on its campus called Johnston College. Johnston focused on humanistic psychology, and the dean thought this is where I'd find my place. I very quickly did. Some of the faculty there were very open to the spiritual perspective I was bringing. The way I wove together psychology and religion, East and West, and the theoretical and the experiential blended in well with their other courses. In particular, what I added to their existing academic studies was integration from the heart instead of the head, from the meditative, not just the analytical. I brought in the spiritual, not just the religious, and the Hasidic, not just the more conventional Jewish approaches. I made good connections with several professors who were open to my teaching a class, and they asked me to write a course description. This is what I wrote:

"The madder you get, the madder you get."—Ken Kesey

"It doesn't matter that it doesn't matter."—Don Juan

Intra-Realities: Awakening and Transition

Once, man stood naked before an immense barren desert that demanded to be crossed. But, underestimating the strength of his nakedness, he declined the challenge, choosing rather to build a society that would provide for a road across the desert. As society grew, man forgot about the desert. Even those who deluded themselves into thinking that they were working on the road found that they were really only working on a chain gang. It seemed as if the effort was no longer to build a society that would forge a way across the desert, but simply to cover up any sign of the desert.

And so the time was filled with empty goals, false gods, reruns, hall passes, Proposition 19s, and junk mail. But one day you go to your mailbox, pull down the flap door, bend down to look into it—and it's empty, and you can look right through it. And there on the other side is the desert again.

So you say, "All right!" and you determine to set out on your own just as soon as you've gotten everything together that you need, because, after all, you're still naked and the desert is still barren. But that won't work either, because there's no end to the supplies that you think you need for your journey. No, it's got to be now. You cannot be free until you leave the oppression behind you—not one moment sooner.

The other side of fear is awe; and the struggle between the naked and the barren is really a dance.

Dreams, plans, and hopes, however beautiful and sincere, are only painkillers and opiates if you are still oppressed, in bondage, and, in all truth, a political prisoner in the system. But a dream outside the prison, even in the desert, is a Divine chariot that can carry you anywhere.

It is time to awaken to these realities; it is time to seek out alternative realities; it is a time for transition and transformation. It is time for new ways.

"Whatever you do may be a way to Me, provided you do it in such a manner that it leads you to Me."—God, according to Martin Buber

"Open your heart to goodness; resist evil karma; and follow the righteous path. Remember truth and know there is no way to peace, peace is the way."—bathroom graffiti in Israel

"But if we desire to make the most of the opportunity that this life gives us, if we wish to respond adequately to the call we have received and to attain the goal we have glimpsed, not merely advance a little towards it, it is essential that there should be an entire self giving. The secret of success in yoga is to regard it not as one of the aims to be pursued in life, but as the whole of life."—Sri Aurobindo

"Listen, listen, listen to my heart's song. Listen, listen, listen to my heart's song. I will never forget you, I will never forsake you. I will never forget you, I will never forsake you."—song of Swami Yogananda

Join us for a class that will challenge who you think you are and where you think you're going.

The description elicited a good response—the classroom was packed and overflowing—and my career as a teacher of spirituality was launched. I became a member of the adjunct faculty at Johnston College and added classes on meditation, Jung, yoga, and one called "The Meaning of Everything." I also taught classes in Judaism and Jewish mysticism. So much was possible on this campus, which was wonderfully supportive.

We were stretching the bounds of humanistic psychology, when a guest lecturer, Jim Fadiman, heard what we were doing. "This is transpersonal psychology." He said, "Why don't you offer a BA in it?" As intriguing as this sounded, all of us at Johnston College said, "What's transpersonal psychology?"

Jim explained to us that the levels of psychological development are reflected in the main schools of psychology: most basic was behavioral psychology—the stimulus response and conditioning of B. F. Skinner. This deals with a more mechanical and physical model of human behavior. Psychoanalytical psychology—the ego, superego and id of Freudian theory—dealt with the emotional and mental workings that are below the surface of our observable behavior. The next level was humanistic psychology—the values and drives towards self-fulfillment articulated by Carl Rogers, who chronicled the goals of a well-functioning human being. Lastly is transpersonal psychology, which transcends the personality to include the soul, or, as Abraham Maslow said, which seeks "the farthest reaches of human nature."

"*That's* what you're doing here," Jim said. "You're integrating body, emotion, mind, and spirit." And with that, the first accredited undergraduate program in transpersonal psychology began.

Many of us who were pioneering these studies were invited to become founding members of the Association of Transpersonal Psychology, and to attend its first annual conference. The prime focus of the conference was blending transpersonal psychology with therapy. My colleagues from Johnston and I presented workshops in transpersonal education. In addition, I led morning sessions where we chanted meditative songs from many traditions.

Johnston College provided me with my first place back in the West where I could meld my experiences with teachings. Transpersonal psychology gave me my true home for many years to come. It's where I began my real work—infusing transpersonal psychology with Jewish mysticism. My singing and teaching could now take wing.

32

THE BIRDS:
A Blessing of the
Universe

As had happened to me before, not all my teachers came in human form. My dormitory apartment was nicely furnished with couches in the living room, a small, round breakfast-room table, and a couple of chairs. The bedroom had a bed and bedside table. It was much more than I needed or than I was accustomed to. My favorite feature was a big sliding glass door that opened from the living room onto a nice grassy area with a big tree.

Sitting on the couch one day, I heard a bird screeching quite loudly. Curious about all the excitement, I went outside and saw a big blue jay hopping up and down the tree, squawking away. I didn't see a cat or dog or any other animal that could have caused such a commotion. Then I looked down on the grass, and there, two baby birds with hardly any feathers on them were peeping for their mother. Now I understood: They had fallen out of the nest and their mother couldn't get them back up.

I knew they were in danger from cats, so I stepped outside. If the babies saw me towering over them, maybe that would scare them to hop back to their mother and the nest. But as I moved toward them, they hopped up my leg and sat on my shoulder. So I walked back indoors, thinking that would scare them off of me and back to their mother. Wrong again. They just sat on my shoulders. They weren't going anywhere.

Meanwhile, the mother bird was flying around, screeching. I finally got the message. She was yelling at *me,* saying, "Take care of them! Take care of them!" I tried to explain to her that I had a busy schedule, but she wouldn't take "no" for an answer. With one last "caw" she took off.

Calling one of my students who wanted to become a veterinarian, I told her what had happened and asked whether she would take care of them. She came half an hour later with a jar of freshly mashed fruits and an eye dropper. She took hold of one of the birds, shoved the dropper into its mouth and squeezed the fruit mush down its throat.

"It's real simple," she told me. "You just have to do this every hour or so for the next several days and they'll be fine."

"That's great," I said. "Take them and take good care of them."

"No," she said, "remember what you taught us about how God sends to each person just what that person needs. They came to *you,* David. You have to take care of them."

Don't you hate it when your teachings come back to you?

Well, I managed to fulfill all my teaching obligations, *and* still get back home in time to feed my babies. What was initially a hassle turned into a real gift. At first, I was running in and out, but soon I began letting go of the unnecessary. These baby jays slowed me down and helped me sort out what I really needed to do. I became more and more present, more in the now. What was at first a fast-food service for the baby birds turned into a full-service activity for slowing me down.

After feeding them, I took out my guitar and sang to them while they sat on my shoulder. Sometimes they even sat on the guitar. They would nestle in my beard or my hair, and put their beak right into my ears and cheep quietly and contentedly. Their mother would come by regularly, calling out to check up on them. "*Caw!* How are they doing? *Caw!* How are they doing?" I'd hold them up for her to see, and she would fly away, reassured.

After a few days, when they were a little older and bigger, I began holding them in my palm, raising and lowering them, teaching them to flap their wings and fly. They would stay airborne for just a few seconds.

I wrote them this song:

You are a blessing of the Universe, God-sent to make us free.
You are a blessing of the Universe, God-sent to make us free.
Singing look at me, look at me—I'll set you free.
Singing look at me, look at me—I'll set you free.

I had really grown to love this godsend and to appreciate how they had changed the rhythm of my life. But one day their mother was calling outside again. I held them up for her to see, but she kept right on screeching. It took me a while to absorb her message this time: she knew they had grown and she wanted them back. I stepped outside and walked over to their tree. The two babies hopped from my shoulder onto the lowest branch, and their mother hopped, flapped, and guided them back up to the higher branch where their nest was.

I went back inside and experienced my first empty-nest syndrome.

Years later, I realized the song wasn't "for the birds," but that it could be sung to all sorts of significant people in our lives.

33

TONY SUTICH:
The Hidden Founder of
Transpersonal Psychology

Carl Rogers was quite famous as the founder of humanistic psychology. But Tony Sutich, the man who worked closely with Carl and was behind the *Journal of Humanistic Psychology*, was virtually unknown.

As Abraham Maslow emerged from humanistic psychology to pioneer the transpersonal psychology movement, it was Tony Sutich who did much of the redefining, clarifying, and distinguishing between humanistic and transpersonal, but behind the scenes. He edited the *Journal of Transpersonal Psychology* and was the backroom visionary for the new Association of Transpersonal Psychology. And he did all this lying flat on his back on a gurney in his home, essentially immobilized from the neck down since he was a teenager, when a baseball injury caused an unusual form of arthritis. Tony was a giant of a man, of a thinker, and of a visionary.

When I first visited Tony, he was on his gurney. A phone was cradled on his pillow, snug to his ear; papers and books lay on an angled table over his chest. He still had enough movement left in his arms so he could pull a cord that answered or hung up the phone or turned pages of the books on the table. Over his head a mirror was positioned at a 45-degree angle. As I sat behind him and looked into the mirror, I had such eye-to-eye contact with him that it was almost like he was sitting right in front of me.

Tony's eyes were alive and filled with joy, his face almost always lit up by a smile. His soul illuminated his whole being with a positive, life-affirming attitude. I soon discovered that he wasn't just a writer and an editor. He was also a therapist. His ability to function only from the neck up put many people's problems into perspective. But it was his ability to connect you to your own soul—beyond the limitations and dramas of the body and ego—that was his true healing capacity and gift.

Knowing Tony was a privilege. His encouragement—for my path of the heart and my own development of transpersonal *education*—came from an ability to see the bigger picture and to understand the need for learning that involved body, emotion, mind, and spirit. He was immensely supportive of my own role in these new programs, although I didn't have the MA or PhD that almost everyone else had. He was my personal accrediting bureau, giving me credit for my years out in the experiential world.

Years later, when Tony passed away, I was driving to his memorial service in Palo Alto. The day was a mix of clouds and rain and sunshine, and the flowers were opening to receive the rain and the sun. Just like Tony, everything in life was for the good of all. I wrote this song as I came to say farewell:

Well the flowers are opening
And the clouds they are opening
To the rain and to the sun
To all the ways of the One.

This too shall pass
This too shall pass
Like the moon on the rise,
Like the look in your eyes.

34

EGO AND SELF:
"I Am the Ambassador of
the Self/Soul"

I was teaching a class on Jungian psychology at Johnston College in 1973. I was the son of a Jungian, and had met Jung. I'd read many books by him, seen him being interviewed on film, and had been through some Jungian therapy. So teaching him made sense. Still, articulating the theories that I had absorbed by osmosis was not so easy.

One day, a student asked whether I could give a clearer definition of ego and Self than what I'd already offered them. I presented several definitions, quoted Jung on the topic, and drew some diagrams on the blackboard. I explained how the personality—the ego—is the mask through which the Self or Soul can express itself, but that you are not your ego any more than an actor is the role he's playing.

I quoted Jung: "For five hundred years man has known that planet Earth is *not* the center of the solar system. But when will man understand that the ego is not the center of the Self?" I taught them from one of Jung's unpublished transcripts: "The ego is the visibility of Self in Time and Space." He described a dialogue between the ego and the Self where the ego was telling the Self/Soul not to push too hard. "You don't understand about everyday life and its demands, taxes, army service, and the like. If you push too hard, you'll push me right over. But then where will you be? Because I'm your feet, and without me you cannot stand up in this world." Jung went on to say that the ego was vital for the Self to give expression.

All this was still too theoretical for the class. It wasn't experiential enough. It wasn't real. I put down the chalk and closed the books I was reading from.

I began to speak: "My name is David Zeller. I am his ego, but I'm not really David, *I'm just the ambassador of his Self.*" As the words flowed through me, I let go of trying to make sense intellectually. "I try to represent him as best as I can, but it's not easy. There are so many other things I have to take care of and pay attention to.

"When an ambassador comes from a foreign country, he has to learn the language, and maybe dress differently. He has to learn about the appropriate electrical current and the monetary currency, locate schools and markets, and learn the lay of the land. You have to learn the ways people address one other, formally and informally. In fact, there's so much to manage that often I forget to represent my own country—my Self.

"But when I slow down just a little," and here I began speaking much more slowly, "and remember who I really am, and who I really represent, I can begin to let my Self sound through me. 'Speak for your Self!' we're told. It's easier said than done."

As I spoke, my ego faded out and my Self came through. I felt a dramatic change in the classroom. There was a presence, a connectedness, a relatedness. It was the best demonstration of ego and Self, and of Self and Soul.

Later, while readjusting to the West, I wrote a letter to Sri Pad, telling him how hard it was to maintain my spiritual practices amid all the distractions and temptations of the material world I was living in. In India, it was so much easier to stay focused on God, and on my own "Blessed Self." (Sri Pad began all his letters with the salutation "Blessed Self," rather than

"Dear So-and-So.") It was a long, whiny letter: my ego was crying over all the obstacles and difficulties.

When I was done, I read the letter. It was embarrassing, a sign of such weakness and struggle. Should I throw it out and start over again? Or write a happy *"Baruch HaShem* (Blessed is God), everything is great!" letter?

I grabbed another piece of paper, took a deep breath, and looked deeper within myself. This time, I wrote a letter from my Self, from my Soul. I wrote about myself in the third person. "David is struggling with this, and is having a hard time with that.... But he's really doing quite well meeting the challenges, and I (the Soul) am fine and still watching over him, and not getting totally ignored by him.... "

I sent both letters to Sri Pad. Together, they were an honest self-appraisal from both sides of my Being.

As long as I could recognize and give expression to both parts of myself, I felt that I could carry on. Some people say the "trans" of transpersonal means "beyond" the personal. I've always taught that the "trans" is from "translucent," that it means "through." To me, the work has always been to bring that which is *beyond* the personal, *through* the personal. Bring it into this everyday world.

In fact, this was another reason I was drawn to Judaism. Judaism says we must not leave or detach from this world in order to come closer to God. We must bring God into this world, and into the everyday, and that we have one day each week to lift the everyday up to God: the Sabbath.

35

CARLOS CASTANEDA:
A Separate Reality

I was becoming more confident in blending my various worlds together, although it was still hard to explain the life I'd had in India with swamis and gurus and miracles almost every day. It was so different from anything people here could imagine. And then I read Carlos Castaneda's second book, *A Separate Reality.*

Carlos was a doctoral student at UCLA who was studying sorcerers and medicine men among the Yaqui Indians of northwestern Mexico. Carlos found a wise old teacher—Don Juan. Rather than study these Indians as an outside observer, as the "scientific" method would "require," he was initiated into their customs, practices, and way of thinking. Don Juan taught him how to become a sorcerer, a man of knowledge. Carlos's books were very controversial. Academics disparaged them because he had joined from inside instead of observing from outside. Other critics claimed that Don Juan was a complete fabrication. Still others were aghast that he seemed to be advocating the use of hallucinogenics.

Personally, I loved the first book. I read it before starting out on my travels to Israel and India. And now its sequel, *A Separate Reality,* just hit the spot. And because so many people had read the book, I could refer to it, and then lead them to *my* separate reality in India. It gave me a language that really enhanced my communication. For instance, Don Juan spoke about the value of being detached in this manner:

" ... a man can learn to see.... Upon learning to see, a man becomes everything by becoming nothing. He, so to speak, vanishes and yet he's there.... Seeing has already detached him from absolutely everything he knew before."

"The sole idea of being detached from everything I know gives me the chills," I [Carlos] said.

"You must be joking! The thing which should give you the chills is not to have anything to look forward to but a lifetime of doing that which you have always done. Think of the man who plants corn year after year until he's too old and tired to get up, so he lies around like an old dog. His thoughts and feelings, the best of him, ramble aimlessly to the only things he has ever done, to plant corn. For me that is the most frightening waste there is.

"We are men and our lot is to learn and to be hurled into inconceivable new worlds."

"Are there any new worlds for us really?" I asked half in jest.

"We have exhausted nothing, you fool," he said impera-tively. "Seeing is for impeccable men. Temper your spirit now, become a warrior, learn to see, and then you'll know that there is no end to the new worlds for our vision."[5]

I was so delighted after reading the book, that I sat down and wrote Carlos a letter.

Dear Carlos,

Thank you for your book. I've just come back from a year living as a sadhu in India, and *A Separate Reality* gave me the language for explaining and sharing a little of what I had received from my teacher and our way of living there.

I'm sure you get lots of letters from all sorts of people, but I'd love to get together to share some of our uncommon experiences.

Also, I'm teaching at a small undergraduate experimental college at the University of Redlands. One of my classes is exploring alternative spiritual realities. Would you consider being a guest lecturer? I'm sure it would be an incredible opportunity for my students to hear from you directly.

I sent the letter to Carlos via the anthropology department at UCLA, with which he was still associated. But I also wondered how many hundreds of letters he must get every week, maybe every day. What were the chances that he'd even see mine, let alone respond to it?

The next week, I was down the hall from the faculty offices when a student came looking for me, saying I had a phone call. As I headed toward the phone, he said it was someone named Carlos Casta-something. Picking up the phone, I heard a voice that sounded very much like the comedian from the 1950s, José Jimenez. "Hello, David? This is Carlos Castaneda. I got your letter, and I could come out tomorrow to meet with you and talk to your class."

Trying to keep my composure, I said, "I'm so glad you called and that you're open to coming to my class. But could we do it next week so I can let the class know in advance?"

"No," he said, "that's the whole idea. I don't want you to let them know. That's not how I work. It's tomorrow or I don't know when.... "

"Okay," I said, "tomorrow it is!"

Carlos surprised me. I had expected someone tough and wiry, weathered and intense. Instead, he was a little roly-poly, more on the soft and warm side, very human and open. Of course, I could only assume that this was, in fact, *the* Carlos Castaneda. His teacher forbade him having any pictures taken or to be at all in the public eye. That was part of his sorcerer's training, part of erasing his personal history.

We spent quite a bit of time exchanging stories. As different as our practice and experience was, we had much to share. We talked a lot about how our teachers taught by putting us through experiences. He told how he was once wearing a sweater that he really loved and Don Juan started pulling on a loose piece of yarn until he had unraveled the entire sweater. Apparently Don Juan did this just to see how Carlos would react. Could he remain detached? Could he maintain a state of mind where nothing mattered?

We walked into the class together, and I said, "Today, we have an unexpected guest, a very special guest—Carlos Castaneda!" Taking in their wonder was a great moment. Hearing Carlos's stories and teachings made for a great class.

We stayed in touch for a number of years. That turned out to be the best proof that it was really him. Or I should say, *he* stayed in touch, because he never gave me a way to reach him directly. But every year or two, I'd invariably be at someone's house for a gathering, the phone would ring, and the call would go out, "David, you've got a phone call. It's Carlos Castaneda!" It always made a great impression. "Hello, David," he'd say, "I just got back from several months in South America. How are you?" And so it went.

Years later, when I moved to Israel, we lost touch. Then I heard that he had passed away. As mysterious as he was, he had been warm and friendly to me, very human and not at all aloof. He was a special soul, so invaluable to have had as a friend along my spiritual journey. His descriptions of the hard work involved in honing the spirit—becoming a "warrior," a "sorcerer," a "hunter," a "man of knowledge" and all his other terms for being on the spiritual path—were deeply profound. As my teachers had passed on to me, he too had been given a map to use to break through aspects of his personality. But the ultimate work was in our own hands. As Carlos wrote in his first book, Don Juan told him, "There are lots of paths. You have to find the path with a heart." That line has stayed with me in all my searching. It was instrumental in how I was drawn or led to my own teachers. My first tape of songs was called "The Path of the Heart." Heart has been at the heart of all my work. It meant so much to me that Carlos and I had that heart connection. There was no other explanation for his calling me from time to time. I'm so glad we were able to share some small part of our separate realities together.

36

Nakasono Sensei: Meeting the Shinto Priest

In the summer of 1973, I was on my way to the annual conference of the Association of Humanistic Psychology, where I was making a presentation on transpersonal education and leading some morning chanting and meditation. That year, it was held in New Orleans. I was driving from Los Angeles, planning to visit my old friend, Thomas Banyacya of the Hopi Indians, in Arizona, then pass through Santa Fe to visit a Japanese Shinto priest, whom a Swiss Jungian therapist, Dora Kalf, had told me about. How she came to know him is a story in itself.

Dora was quite well known for her work in "sand play therapy," a method of working primarily with children that had also proven highly effective with adults. I had seen her when I was a boy in Switzerland. In room after room were shelves from floor to ceiling filled with every imaginable miniature figure and prop with which you could create any kind of "picture" in a shallow, table-sized sandbox, with no limitations imposed because of your inability to draw.

She was researching the stages of psychological development that were emerging, in symbolic form, in this therapeutic process. In the middle of her research, she became very ill and was diagnosed as terminal. Determined to complete her research before she died, she came to this Shinto priest, who had moved from Japan to Paris. As she had done with the symbols of other traditions, she wanted to compare her images of consciousness with Shinto representations. The Shinto religion is one of the most ancient in Japan, much older than Buddhism. It is based on nature and the life force in all things. She presented her findings to him.

"Do you want to talk about your research when you are dying?" he asked.

Quite startled that he "knew" something she was keeping to herself, she said, "There's nothing I can do about it, so I just want to continue my research."

"Do you want to get well?" he asked.

"Of course, but the doctors said there was nothing that can be done."

"If you want to get well, then let's get to work."

And he healed her.

While visiting the priest after he had moved to Santa Fe, he let Dora observe as he administered acupuncture to a young girl who was paralyzed from the waist down. As he put his needles into her foot, the girl screamed in pain. Dora couldn't bear to stay in the room. Later that week, she ran into the parents at the post office in town. She approached them, trying to apologize for leaving in the middle of the treatment. "I'm so sorry I left, it was just too.... "

"Yes, wasn't it remarkable?" they said with joy. "Just a week ago, she couldn't feel anything in her feet!"

So when Dora heard my story of my spiritual journey in India, she thought that he might be someone I would like to meet.

On the outskirts of Santa Fe, I called Nakasono Sensei, the Shinto priest, introduced myself, and inquired whether I might stop over for a short visit. He was delighted and invited me right over. His home was a combination of Western and Eastern, with both chairs and pillows. He sat on a cushion on the floor. His eyes were soft and warm.

After introducing ourselves, he asked whether I was Jewish, which sort of surprised me. I was not Orthodox at the time. Nor did I dress in a "Jewish way." But I did mention that I had lived in Israel for two years before being a sadhu in India.

He said that in his Shinto religion there was an interesting story in their oral tradition. He asked whether I knew what oral tradition was. I assured him I knew what oral tradition meant (that much I had heard about in Judaism). And this is what he told me:

> According to Shinto oral tradition, great spiritual teachers met several thousand years ago to report on the progress of their various missions: Had they succeeded in leading various peoples around the world to a spiritual awakening and evolution? Many of them reported of their success through the wisdom of the Vedas in India, and the wisdom of the *Tao Te Ching* and the *I Ching* in China, and the wisdom of the Aztecs in South America, and so on. Everyone felt quite good, almost certain that they'd accomplished their specific assignments. But one person raised a troubling question.
>
> "Wasn't our mission to lead people through a material awakening *and* a spiritual awakening, and then bring the two together? If it was just a spiritual process, why did we even need to come into this material world? Our task was to bring the two—material and spiritual—*together.*"
>
> "You're right," said the group's leader. "We were supposed to lead people first through a material awakening, then a spiritual one, then unite them. But who among you will take this on?"
>
> No one wanted that responsibility. These were all enlightened people. They knew that a material awakening could only be reached by going through possessiveness, competition, aggression, violence, and war, and no one wanted to do that.

"No volunteers?" asked the leader. "Then I'll have to choose someone."

"So," said Nakasono Sensei, pausing briefly and looking straight at me, "the chosen people—were the Jews." Then he went on with his story:

From then on, all spiritual traditions were split between the exoteric and the esoteric, between the mundane and the secret, between religious dogma and spiritual experience. Because, Sensei explained, if people knew only about the spiritual reality, they would not be motivated to develop the material world and to synthesize these two realms.

The tablets of the Ten Commandments became the universal, and particularly the Jewish, symbol of this process: Spirit inscribed in Stone. Spirit in Matter.

The Shinto priest turned to me. "You know," he said, "in the Shinto tradition we have *five* energy centers in our body. The first center, at the level of the genitals, represents life and death. The second, at the level of the navel, represents power. The third center, at the heart, represents emotions. The fourth, at the throat, represents intellect. And the fifth center, at the forehead, represents the spiritual. All these represent levels of consciousness. Each center has a sound associated with it. The center at the genitals has the sound "AH," the navel "OH," the heart "OO," the throat "AY," and the forehead "EE." In ancient Japan, the samurai, the martial artists, indicated the level of their mastery by adding the sound of that energy center to the end of their title.

"But in ancient Japan," Sensei told me, "the word for 'samurai' was *mosh*. So if someone was just beginning, and had only mastered the lowest center, he was called 'Mosh-AH.' Someone who had reached the level of control of the power center at the navel was called 'Mosh-OH.' If you mastered the heart center, you were called 'Mosh-OO.' And a master of the intellectual center, of speech and expression, was called 'Mosh-AY.'

"You know, 'Mosh-ay' is Hebrew for 'Moses!'" my Shinto priest exclaimed. "Moses was on that high level to bring down the stone tablets of Spirit in Matter, and to teach and give expression to all God's instructions."

He didn't say this next step, but it occurred to me that the level of the forehead, the spiritual level, would be 'Mosh-EE'— which would be the level of 'Mosh-ee-ach,' which is Hebrew for the Messiah.

The Shinto priest went on to explain, very excitedly, that if you bring energy down from the highest center to the lowest and back up again to the highest, going through the sounds of each center, you get the sound of the Four-Lettered Name of God, the Tetragrammaton. A little nervous, I tried to explain that, in our Jewish tradition, we do not pronounce that name. It could be seen as similar to nuclear energy: very powerful and, when used irresponsibly, very dangerous. In addition, we have the mystical understanding that each time we see the *Name* of God, we should try to re-create the *experience* of God.

Sensei continued, "Jews did a wonderful job developing the material. Wonderful job! But they forgot about the spiritual. If you don't bring the spiritual and the material together, the whole world will blow up! I don't care, I'm ready to go!" he laughed. "My job is just to remind Jews what their job is."

I was quite stunned by this story and its message. But I'd been around the world, studying many of the world traditions, so I said, "That's very well and good, but Jews aren't the only people worried about the future and its dire consequences. The Hopis have a similar message, saying if people don't get their Spirit and Matter together, 'purification day' is coming and everything will burn."

The priest replied in his Japanese-modified English, "Hopi people wonderful people. Hopi religion wonderful religion. But Hopi not responsible for whole world. Jews responsible for whole world."

I said, "The Buddhists speak about the end of days, and the coming of Avalokateshwara, and of our need to achieve higher states of compassion and being."

"Buddhist people wonderful people. Buddhist religion wonderful religion. Buddhist not responsible for whole world. Jews responsible for whole world."

I went through Christian, Hindu, and Sufi teachings, and several others. To each, Sensei answered, "Wonderful people, wonderful religion. But not responsible for whole world. Jews responsible for whole world."

I didn't hear him saying that Judaism was better than these other faiths. Rather, I understood that each people and tradition had been chosen to do a particular task for all of humanity. Just as each organ in our body must fulfill its "destiny" and function for the overall health of the whole body, so each religious tradition has its function in the body of humankind.

I came away from this conversation with a new understanding of the Commandments, and a new appreciation for Judaism. It was really quite unique from many other religions, especially by insisting that we live in the material world *and* in the spiritual world. No monasteries. No retreating from the world. Rather a day-to-day life filled with practices that can unite each material act with spiritual intention.

The word *mitzvah,* is usually translated as "commandment." It can also be translated as "to join together." We are "en-joined" to live in such a way that we constantly join Heaven and Earth, Spirit and Matter. Acting in such a sacred manner joins us to God; God is One with us, and God flows through us in everything we do.

No retreat? I must correct myself. Judaism gives us a spiritual retreat once a week—the Sabbath. Six days a week, we work to bring an aspect of the spiritual into the everyday material. One day a week, we strive to bring the material into the spiritual. In between our spiritual activities of prayers, rituals, and ceremonies, we have the material through wonderful meals spiced with inspirational learning and song.

If the Ten Commandments are Spirit in Matter, then our Sabbath is Matter in Spirit. Together, they keep our lives balanced.

Now, years later, I see God's great compassion. At that point in my life, had I heard this teaching of the Jews' responsibility for the world from a Jew, let alone a rabbi, I would have stood up and not very politely denounced his chosen-people-ness and walked out. But God, the Compassionate One, sent a Shinto priest to tell the story. From *him,* I could hear it. I owe much to my Jewish teachers and rebbes for helping me become who I am today. But I also owe a great deal to my Shinto priest, and, of course to the Holy Blessed and Compassionate One.

37

REB ZALMAN SCHACHTER:
Professor, Translator, and Explorer

When I returned to the U.S. from India, I knew that my Jewish spiritual experiences would help me bridge the Eastern and the psychological. I knew Shlomo was my rebbe and my primary connection to the heart and depth of Judaism. But he spoke a fairly exclusive language of Judaism, with little attention to the language of the East or to psychology and meditation. In fact, that is why I was so drawn to him. He just went straight to "the deepest of the deep," as he would call it. All of my closest teachers were submerged pretty exclusively in their own tradition. It was through that depth within their *own* path that they connected to all the universal truths.

Still, I needed someone who could help me with the "translation." As Carlos had provided a general terminology for the path, I needed a teacher who could say that what is called "enlightenment" in Eastern traditions was called a "state of prophesy," or *Ruach HaKodesh*, "Holy Spirit," in Judaism. That's when I began hearing about Rabbi Zalman Schachter (now known as Rabbi Zalman Schachter-Shalomi). Here was someone who was raised deep in the Orthodox, Hasidic world, whose interest and experience in mysticism led *him* to explore outside Orthodoxy and even into other religious teachings and practices. Reb Zalman, along with being a rebbe, was a professor. He was a professor in different universities, including Temple and Naropa, but I mean it in the sense that he taught in more "academic," organized bundles of knowledge—learning a subject, analyzing it, and storing it for future reference. And he was always a student: He loved studying other wisdoms and meeting teachers from various paths and practices.

Having been into many other traditions myself, I needed Zalman as my *targeman,* my "translator," who would integrate me back into Judaism. But Shlomo remained my rebbe—the caretaker of my soul. Both were very precious to me and both played important roles in my progress. Shlomo could take me into a different world through his songs, stories, and teachings, while Zalman, the professor, could give a five-day lecture series or workshop on *topics* like Kabbalah or counseling the soul.

In fact, the workshop Zalman did for our Transpersonal Institute around 1976 was the most in-depth, concise, organized, and inspiring learning I have ever had on the inner workings of Kabbalah. Especially useful was how he wove Kabbalah into a psychological model that was meaningful for all of us.

At one evening session where Shlomo and Zalman were teaching together, someone asked a question while Shlomo was in the middle of teaching something "very deep," as he called it. Shlomo stopped, tilted his head up toward the heavens, then rolled his eyes back as he "brought down" the answer he was "receiving." Zalman jumped into the middle of all this. "Shloimele," he said, "where did you go when you rolled your eyes back?!" Shlomo couldn't really answer. He just did it; he just went there. Zalman wanted to map the territory and identify the terrain. Shlomo was content just going there, which he did with ease.

Davening with Zalman on Shabbat, I was surprised by how familiar I felt with the melodies of the Hebrew prayers until I realized he was using "Scarborough Fair," and the "Umbrellas of Cherbourg," or some Bob Dylan song. Rosh HaShanah was done in a workshop mode. We had work lists, and dialogued with each other and in small groups, trying to get to the root of some of the stuck places in our personality that we really wanted to change. Shlomo never had printed sheets to hand out. Zalman always did.

In transpersonal psychology and the consciousness community, a common expression was the search for the "paradigm shift." This is the level at which seemingly opposite or incompatible things are suddenly perceived as harmonious and compatible. While I was working to make the "paradigm shift," the leap of consciousness and spirituality, *within* Orthodox Judaism, Zalman had made his peace making the paradigm shift *outside*. He was already planting seeds with the Aquarian Minyan of Berkeley and the Boston Havura that would sprout up all over as the Jewish Renewal movement. I felt like we met at "the wall," not the Western Wall, but the Wall of Orthodoxy: me climbing in, and Zalman climbing out. I, the ex-sadhu with very little (of the tradition) to carry, and Zalman, the rebbe/scholar, with lots of precious cargo: the tremendous knowledge of the tradition and all its craft. He had so much in him from the depths of Judaism, and I have always been grateful for what I could learn from him. His teachings on "the Four Worlds" of Kabbalah have been the cornerstone of many of my own teachings blending Judaism, transpersonal psychology, and holistic health: body, emotion, mind, and spirit.

38

REB SHLOMO:
How Do You Teach Torah When You're Angry with God?

In 1974, there was a conference—"Torah and Dharma"—in Berkeley, California, focusing on the connections between Judaism and other traditions like Sufism, Zen Buddhism, and Yoga. Representatives of the different traditions were invited, including Reb Shlomo and Reb Zalman. Shlomo, as often happened, was double-booked and couldn't come. There were keynote talks, smaller seminars, and panel discussions. The final panel had all the teachers together for the last questions and answers.

Someone in the audience asked *the* question: "It appears to me that the Sufis, the Yogis, and the Zen teachers on our panel are all Jewish! Can anyone explain what's going on?"

There was a murmur from the audience and from the panel. Zalman rose to the occasion. "Before I left for the conference, I called up Reb Shlomo and said, 'Shloimele, I'm about to go to the conference in Berkeley. I know you really wanted to be there, too. Do you have anything you want to say to them? The tape recorder is hooked up to the phone and recording.' And this is what he said in answer to your question." And with that Zalman pressed the start button on a tape recorder sitting on the table in front of him.

This is a paraphrase of what Shlomo said. It is one of those classic teachings of his that I have been retelling ever since:

My sweetest friends, I'm so sorry I couldn't be with you for this holy gathering, but I'd like to share with you one thought I have, so please open your hearts. The Torah teaches that a Cohen, a priest, must remain in a state of purity if he is to serve God in the Holy Temple. Among the things that would disqualify him was contact with a dead body. The question arises: What was the nature of the impurity? Did the dead body have cooties or carry disease? It appears that the problem was quite different. The impurity stemmed from the confrontation with death: its concept and its reality and the thoughts and feelings around it.

Coming in touch with death, a person can't help thinking, "What kind of God makes a world with death in it? If I were God, I'd do things very different; I'd do things better."

Let's put it this way. When you come in contact with death, you can't help being a little angry with God. And if you are a Cohen, how can you be angry in your heart with God, and then go into the Holy Temple to serve Him? It just doesn't go. So the priest had to wait until sunset, and take a *mikvah*, a ritual bath, and then he could return to serve God the next day.

These laws of the priesthood regarding serving God became the basis for many of the Jewish laws of mourning. If your father or mother, brother or sister, son or daughter, husband or wife died, from the time of their death until they are buried, you are technically exempt from most positive commandments. For example, you don't have to say blessings, because that's a form of thanking and serving God, and right now, you may be in a frame of mind of being a little bit angry with God. So you aren't obligated to say those blessings.

And you know, my sweetest friends, today we don't have a Beit HaMikdash, a Holy Temple, and although we still have Cohanim, priests, we don't have animal or incense offerings to serve God in the Holy Temple. Today we serve God through offerings of words of Torah study and words of prayer. Today our rabbis are like our priests, serving God through teaching Torah. But if you are angry with God, you can't teach Torah. You can say the words, but the love and light within them do not flow through them.

So please open your hearts. The saddest thing is that today our teachers and rabbis haven't just touched one dead person. They've been touched by Six Million dead people. And they are so angry with God, so angry with God. *Gevald*, are they angry with God! And because they are so angry with God, all their words of Torah are just that: words. There's no light, no taste, no meaning, no melody in them.

But young people today are so hungry for that light, for that meaning, for that melody—for the deepest inner dimensions of truth. And if they can't get it from Judaism, they'll go anywhere that love and light are to be found.

Thank God our hungry, searching, younger generation found some traditions that weren't so angry with God, and they could get the love and light and meaning that they so craved. And today in Judaism, *Baruch HaShem*, thank God, we have a whole new generation of teachers who haven't been touched directly by the Six Million (or maybe they have taken Six Million *mikvahs* from tears of sadness and then another Six Million *mikvahs* from tears of joy). And their words are filled with light and joy and love.

God willing, now people can come back to Judaism to quench that deep, powerful, longing for God's love and light through teachings, prayers, songs, and dances from our own tradition. I bless us all that we should find that beauty in Torah, in Shabbos, and in the deepest depths of the heart of our holy and ancient and living tradition.

Thank you so much. God bless you all. Good Shabbos, Good Shabbos.

Zalman pushed the stop button on his tape recorder. And we all had Shlomo's answer recorded before the conference commenced and before the question was asked. As I recall, the room was very quiet as we all absorbed this profound teaching.

39

REB GEDALIAH KENIG:
Sh'ma Yisrael

As I continued making headway in transpersonal psychology, I was also advancing in Judaism. I often went to the Bay Area to see Shlomo or Zalman when they came out from the East Coast, and occasionally Shlomo came to Los Angeles. Best of all were trips to Israel for the summer every year or two. There, I studied with Shlomo and Zalman at Shlomo's cooperative community, his moshav. I even taught a little from my experiences in Jewish meditation. But I was still looking for someone else to fill in some missing piece in my range of Jewish teachers.

After my life-changing Jewish experiences in India, I made a deal with God. I said, "I'll go down the Jewish path, and I'll take it on fully. Like my teachers in India, I will be faithful to the depth of my own tradition. But, God, could You please show me someone in the Jewish world today who is as quiet, deep, and present as many of the teachers I met in India?" For all their depth and their soul, Shlomo and Zalman were so much in *this* world. I knew Judaism was about being in this world, joining Spirit and Matter, but there had to be other ways to do it, with more constant connectedness and peacefulness and sense of oneness.

I finally found that person—Reb Gedaliah Kenig. I met him for the first time around 1975. He was teaching a class in his home in Meah Sha'arim, in the heart of Jerusalem's Hasidic world. Reb Gedaliah was very quiet, very soft-spoken, very unassuming. Though only in his early fifties, he was an old soul. I later discovered he was considered one of the leaders of the community of Rebbe Nachman of Breslov, in Israel. Rebbe Nachman (1772–1810) was the great-grandson of the Baal Shem Tov, the founder of the Hasidic movement.

Reb Gedaliah was speaking in Hebrew to a large group of people squeezed around his dining room table. That was unusual, because most ultra-Orthodox rabbis only taught in Yiddish. That tended to exclude most modern Israelis, since they ordinarily spoke only Hebrew. He was teaching from a text called *Likutei Moharan* ("Gleanings of Our Holy Teacher") that had the most essential teachings of Rebbe Nachman. To paraphrase, he was saying something like:

> Seventy children and grandchildren of Jacob descended into Egypt. They are the seeds of the seventy [archetypal] nations of the world and its seventy languages. And sometimes a person must wander through many nations and many languages until he finally hears his own soul crying out to him. And when at last he hears his soul crying out, what does he hear?—"*Sh'ma Yisrael, HaShem Elokaynu, HaShem Echad,*" "Hear, O Israel, The Lord Is Our God, The Lord Is One."

I had never met this man before. Yet he was giving over a teaching of Rebbe Nachman, written in the early 1800s, that described the experience that had happened to me just a few years earlier in India. He was telling *my* story. But most important, he was the answer to my prayer. Reb Gedaliah, like his teacher before him, Rabbi Avraham Steinhartz, was deeply committed to reaching out and loving each and every Jew. He was active as the leader of his community and in collecting and writing the teachings of his mentors. He was teaching in the Breslov yeshivas and developing a new Breslov community project in Sefat. And he did it all with presence, depth, quiet peacefulness, and love.

153

People sometimes ask me how I knew he was one of my rebbes. I answer simply that there was more of me at the table when I sat with him than when I sat with most others. I was more whole, and he saw me as so much more than I could see or know myself. It was years before I could access by myself some of those places of knowing and feeling that he took me to when I learned with him. Shlomo also took me there, but there was something in Reb Gedaliah's nature and presence—or maybe simply that he wasn't running all over the world like Shlomo and interacting with everyone—that touched something so deep within me. Just like the *Sh'ma* I heard in India.

40

REB GEDALIAH:
The Tefillin and the Bus

After my transforming experience of the *Sh'ma* at the Sri Aurobindo Ashram, I had found a Hebrew prayer book in the library there. I sat down, happy that I knew enough Hebrew from my two years in Israel and my time with Shlomo to write down prayers and blessings to include in my morning meditation.

From the morning blessings I particularly loved two prayers that were said, the first after putting on the head tefillin just above the third eye: "And from Your wisdom, Supernal God, emanate to me; and from Your understanding, give me discernment; and with Your loving-kindness increase upon me; and with Your strength cut off my adversaries and rebels. And may You pour goodly oil on the seven branches of the menorah to cause Your goodness to flow to Your creatures. You open Your hand and satisfy the desire of every living being." The second prayer was said when wrapping the tefillin straps around your finger: "And I will betroth you to Me eternally; and I will betroth you to Me in righteousness, justice, loving-kindness, and compassion; and I will betroth you to Me in faith; and you shall know [have consciousness of] God" (Hos. 2:21–22).

Relating to God as the Beloved in marriage was very appealing to me. Since I didn't have any tefillin in India, I imagined putting them on; then, I would say those prayers and the *Sh'ma,* and meditate.

Back in the United States, I found my old tefillin from my bar mitzvah. I wasn't ready to put them on every day, but when "the spirit moved me," I put them on and meditated while wearing them.

Then one day, someone broke into my off-campus apartment in Redlands. Among the things missing was my tefillin. Realizing that "the Lord giveth and the Lord taketh away," I assumed that God was telling me I didn't need them. So I didn't pursue the issue.

Then I went back to Israel for the summer to be with Reb Shlomo and Reb Zalman. Sitting with Zalman one afternoon, I said, "You know, I used to have tefillin, and put them on from time to time, but I was a little uncomfortable because they were made of leather, and I've been a vegetarian for many years. Then, someone stole them. I figured God was telling me I don't need them. What do you think I should do?"

I am grateful that Zalman did not take it upon himself to solve my dilemma. Turning to me, he said, "That's a question that you should ask Reb Gedaliah! You have such a special connection with him. Go to him."

I was so comfortable talking to Zalman about this, and my vegetarian stuff, and all my California cosmic life. And it was so hard to say things like that to Reb Gedaliah, coming as he did from so deep within the tradition. Zalman was directing me toward a big step.

Reb Gedaliah had made a deep impression on me, having been the answer to my prayer for a deep, present, and compassionate teacher of Judaism. Now was the time to come to him with a big question: Should I replace my stolen tefillin or continue to do without them?

Of course, I knew he would say I have to replace them. But I needed to go through this process so I could understand that

God had taken them away from me because I was so ambivalent about them. It wasn't a question of whether God wanted me to wear them or not. It was a question of whether *I* wanted to do this mitzvah that had been enjoined by God. It was a question of whether I wanted to really be enwrapped with this Godly mitzvah.

Sitting down with Reb Gedaliah, I mumbled through my story of my missing tefillin, and my vegetarian philosophy—this time more embarrassed than when I had mentioned it to Reb Zalman. Reb Gedaliah said, "Of course, you have to put on tefillin. Go *right now* and buy a new pair and come right back!"

I went to a nearby store in Meah Sha'arim, bought new tefillin, and came back to his home. Reb Gedaliah got up, and told me to come with him. He took me to a *mikvah* (ritual bath) near his house, and we submerged ourselves in the purifying waters. When we got outside, he said we should go to the Kotel, the Western Wall of the ancient Holy Temple, and put the tefillin on there.

He asked some people standing at a street corner, "Is the bus coming soon for the Kotel?"

Someone looked at his watch and answered, "No, it won't come for quite a while."

Just then, a private tourist bus pulled up. The door swung open and the driver asked, "Does anyone know how to get to the Kotel from here?"

Reb Gedaliah took me by the hand, pulled me along with him into the bus, and gave the driver directions, this time with us along as passengers.

This was almost identical to the bus ride with Sri Pad. I knew I was in the right hands, in God's hands.

The bus took us right to the entrance to the Kotel. We got off and started walking. Now I was preoccupied with thoughts of Reb Gedaliah putting the tefillin on me in such a public place, and I was getting nervous, wondering whether I had made a mistake. But Reb Gedaliah led me past the outside public area into the darker inside section to the left of the Wall. This was far away from the crowd. There he reminded me of the blessings and assisted me in putting on the tefillin. "Take as long as you want," he said, "I'll be sitting right over there whenever you want me." He sat down on a bench across from me, picked up a holy book, and began learning.

I had been gently reinstated into the mitzvah of tefillin. "And I will betroth you to Me eternally; and I will betroth you to Me in righteousness, justice, loving-kindness, and compassion; and I will betroth you to Me in faith; and you shall know God."

41

PASCAL THEMANLYS: Finding the Mother in Israel

I met Pascal Themanlys in Jerusalem around 1976, through my dear friends Aryeh and Ala Rottenberg. We had met at gatherings with Rabbi Shlomo Carlebach and found we also shared an interest in meditation. They were very involved in a meditation group led by Pascal. The group followed the teachings of Max Mordechai Theon, who had been a Hasid, and a student of the Rebbe of Vorke, who was known as the Stille Rebbe, "the Silent Rebbe," for the deep states of meditative silence that he would enter into with his students. Theon had left the Rebbe's court and went to teach in England, France, and eventually Algeria. Among his followers in France was Pascal's father, David, who passed the teachings and practices on to his son.

One evening, I joined them in Pascal's weekly gathering, where I also shared some of my experiences in Jewish meditation. At these meetings, we sat in a circle, alternating men and women. Before meditating, someone would read or teach from a Jewish mystical text, then this invocation would be read:

> We regard this meditation as part of the holy service; to help build the bridge between this world and the higher worlds.

> We should try to open ourselves to receive blessings, lights, and forces from above, and to develop the spiritual

senses, according to the tradition of the prophets, the kabbalists, and the *tzaddikim*. Especially according to the teaching of the Holy Ari, who used to bring his students to drink living waters from the well of Miriam the prophetess.

Our intention is to sanctify this meditation for the purpose of reaching inner quiet, concentration, and prayer of the heart, and to rest until reaching *dvekut* (union), as did the first Hasidim; for the covenant of rest is part of the secrets of the Sabbath.

We are sitting in the violet light of the Tabernacle of Peace.

The order of the portion of the week in the Book of Genesis hints to the phases in the spiritual ascent:

Bereshit ("In the beginning"); Noah; *Lech Lecha* ("Go thyself"); *Vayera* ("And [God] appeared").

Bereshit—in the mind, wisdom; Noah—rest; *Lech Lecha*, Go to your true Self—the ascent of the soul; *Vayera*—for all the Children of Israel saw the sounds at Mount Sinai.

May He remember us so that His *Shechinah* (Divine Presence) rests upon us;

And may the spirit of wisdom and understanding descend upon us;

And may that which is written concerning us be fulfilled:

"And the spirit of the Lord shall rest upon him,

The spirit of wisdom and understanding,

The spirit of council and might,

The spirit of knowledge and fear of the Lord."

Bereshit Noah—first rest; as it is written, "And you shall be silent."[6]

We meditated silently for twenty minutes. Afterward, we went around the circle, each person sharing his or her experience. Pascal taught that each individual's experience was a product of the whole group dynamic and belonged to everyone.

It was a very sweet and diverse group of people, and we enjoyed sitting and socializing after meditating. Pascal said to me, "I have a picture of Theon's house when he lived in Algeria. Would you like to see it?"

Actually, I really wasn't interested in seeing the picture. But to be polite, I said, "Yes, I'd love to see it."

From a glass cabinet, Pascal took down a very small oil painting of the house. It looked like a splotch of white for the house, with a splotch of red for the roof, and some splotches of green for trees. I didn't know why this was so important to see.

"Oh, that's very nice," I lied.

"Would you like to know who painted the picture?" He asked.

"I could care less," I thought. "What does this guy want from me, anyway?"

But I said, "Yes, I'd love to know who painted this."

"Mirra Alfassa," he said.

"Mirra Alfassa?" I thought. "Who is Mirra Alfassa? And what do I care?"

"Perhaps you knew her as the Mother at the Sri Aurobindo Ashram."

"Oh my God," I said, my eyes popping and my mouth dropping, "please tell me everything you know about Theon and the Mother."

I learned from Pascal that Theon had left Poland and taught Kabbalah and meditation in France and England around the turn of the twentieth century. Apparently, he had influenced some people who went on to become great teachers, including Madam Blavatsky of the theosophical movement and Mirra Alfassa. Some time after Mirra had studied with Theon, she went on holiday with her family to India, where she met Sri Aurobindo in the French province of Pondicherry. She left France and spent the rest of her life in India.

So the story about the Mother that I had first heard from Sister Diana in India was now told from the Jewish side.

Pascal continued, telling how Theon went on to teach and write, and how he and his wife would meditate as a couple, and she would be a channel for some of his teachings, which were also published.

"Would you like to see the books?" he asked.

"I would *really* like to see them!" I said enthusiastically.

He showed me a book, in French. On the title page was Theon's logo—a Jewish star with a rose in the center. I was looking at the source of the symbol of the Sri Aurobindo Ashram that I was still wearing around my neck. In Hebrew, the word *shoshanna* can mean "rose" or "lotus."

This experience reminded me of a story about a simple Jew who lived in a small village. For several nights in a row he had the same dream. He dreamed that under a bridge in Vienna was buried a great treasure. He kept ignoring the dream, but it kept recurring. At last he had to pursue it, and he traveled the long distance to Vienna. He walked around the city, looking at every bridge he could find. And there it was: the bridge in his dream. It was the bridge to the palace of the king. He waited around all day, but there were always lots of people around. And when there weren't any people, then the soldier guarding the bridge was always there.

What to do? He couldn't just start digging, and yet his constant lingering there had already aroused the suspicions of the guard. At last the guard approached him and asked why he was hanging around there. He decided to tell the guard his dream, hoping at least they could split the treasure between them. "I had a dream that under this bridge is a great treasure, so I came here to try to dig it up."

"Fool!" the guard roared with laughter, "You can't chase after every dream. Dreams are a complete nonsense. Why, if I ran after all my wishful dreams, I'd go to a little village, where, in the house of a Jew called Moishele, I'd find a treasure under his stove!" And he laughed again.

Moishele quickly returned home and dug under his stove, and there was the treasure. But if he hadn't followed his dreams and traveled so far, he might never have found the treasure in his own home.

Like Moishele, I had come full circle. I had gone all the way to India to experience the depth of the meaning of the *Sh'ma*, of God's Oneness, the heart of Judaism. I had become a religious Jew, and now here I was in Jerusalem, discovering the treasure under my own hearth.

Once again, I learned that Judaism really has an ancient and deep tradition of meditation. I wasn't just importing and adapting something from the Far East. I wasn't just being excessively self-indulgent. I was plugging into an ancient and living transmission. I also learned that behind even the most seemingly annoying and unrelated questions or conversations (like the one I thought I was having with Pascal), there is a laughing and loving God calling you and me home.

42

ELANA: Bringing Heaven Down to Earth

When I was in India, someone read my palm and my astrological chart and said I'd stay in India and become a swami. I told him I was planning to go back to America, be Jewish, get married, and have children. "Oh, you'll have lots of children," he said, "you'll be in charge of an orphanage!" Well, that wasn't what I had in mind. But where would I find my wife? This was the missing link in integrating the transpersonal and the Jewish. To my delight, she would come to me through a program at the Institute of Transpersonal Psychology (ITP) in Menlo Park, California, where I was associate director and professor.

Once, ITP invited Charlotte Selver and her husband, Charles Brooks, to lead a weekend workshop. Charlotte was the mother of "sensory awareness" and had influenced Fritz Perls, Eric Fromm, and Alan Watts. We opened the weekend to the general public, announcing through the grapevine that this "teacher of teachers" was coming, and that there were limited openings for the public for this special workshop with her.

A few days later, the phone rang at the Institute, and I took the call myself. Someone was inquiring about the workshop: when will it be, how much does it cost, and then, after reserving a place, she asked where it would take place and how to get there. Now, I may have traveled around the world, and I may have developed my sensory awareness, but my sense of direction was not my strongest trait. And, the Institute was located in a home at the top of a hill at the end of a long winding road. So I proceeded to give the most detailed directions—the kind *I* would want someone to give *me*, so I couldn't possibly miss a turn and get lost—of every curve in the road and every distinct sign within every two-tenths of a mile or so. After this long and detailed description, the woman at the other end of the phone said in consternation, "Who is this?"

"This is David Zeller, the associate director."

"Oh," she said in surprise and a little embarrassment, "I thought you were a woman."

"No, it's me, but I have a high voice, and many people make that mistake."

"But I should have recognized your voice, because I've heard you talk before, and I'm a speech therapist."

"Where did you hear me before, and how did you learn about this workshop?"

"You sang and spoke last week to the staff at the Stanford University Children's Clinic. I work there."

"Where were you sitting during the presentation?"

"I was sitting on the floor to your right, wearing blue jeans."

"Oh," I said, "you were the one with the pretty green eyes!"

Her name was Elaine Heller (later she switched to her Hebrew name, Ety, and then to Elana). She followed my directions to the workshop, and we followed Charlotte's directions as we worked on our awareness in dyads. Charlotte Selver was a squat old woman, with plain, straight, neck-length gray hair. She used large earphones over her head that were attached to a roving microphone so she could still hear clearly, despite her own deteriorating sense of hearing. She was a commanding presence and she lovingly, sometimes fiercely, guided each individual to be aware of his or her own presence.

Elaine and I became aware together, and we started going out. As a speech therapist, she had primarily worked with children the last few years under a new mentor, Magda Gerber, who taught a unique method of child education called "Educaring." It was based on respect for each child. She called the parent or teacher an "educarer," and taught him or her to respect an infant by talking directly to the child in an adult-like tone, explaining what he or she was about to do, making eye contact, and waiting for the child's response. "The goal," Magda said, "is to help nurture authentic infants who are competent, confident, curious, attentive, exploring, cooperative, secure, peaceful, focused, self-initiating, resourceful, involved, cheerful, aware, interested, and inner-directed."

Elaine had all those characteristics. She also had joy and sparkle. She communicated with everyone—friends and clients—with this same direct approach. Her real love, professionally, was doing speech therapy with adults who had lost their speech due to stroke or trauma. She loved the challenge of helping them discover and create new pathways to reconnect what they knew in their fine minds, but could no longer find the words to express. That was her work before coming out to California, and soon after we got married, she got a new job as director of speech therapy at a nearby community college. But best of all was her application of all she knew about speech development and communication to our own three children as they came along. But I'm jumping ahead.

Elaine had me locked in her radar from the beginning, knowing we were meant for each other. I broke it off a few times; I wasn't used to being zeroed in on like that. I tried various dodges and interruptions with trips to Israel. But she wrote letters and never let me out of her sight. I realized she was right.

Though we met through transpersonal psychology, we blossomed in our shared desire for a richer Jewish life. I was already pretty observant, but I needed someone to go the last mile with me. She had done some Eastern meditation but was trying to find her way into the Jewish community. I introduced her to Shlomo and Zalman, and after many workshops, Shabbats, and a wonderful weekend retreat called "the Joys of Jewishing" with the Aquarian Minyan of Berkeley, we decided to get married. Shlomo and Zalman did our wedding together. The ceremony lasted hours, with much singing, stories, and teachings. Family and friends who were not familiar with Shlomo's long weddings nearly starved until food was served after the ceremony. We had a potluck vegetarian dinner, with one table with food from kosher kitchens, and one table with food from *other* kitchens. It was a low-budget, high-spirited wedding.

Now I had my professional, transpersonal community that Ety became a part of; and we had our personal, religious Shlomo-and-Zalman Jewish community; and *we* also had our own Jewish home. We had many Shabbats and an unforgettable Passover with Shlomo. With lots of people always in our home, and singing and discussions going on for hours, they called our table the "timeless *tish*." *Tish*, Yiddish (*Tisch*, in German) for "table," was traditionally a Hasidic gathering around the table of the rebbe. For us, it was simply all of us being together, losing all sense of time in the magic of Shabbat. Soon we began to have meditations, and our activities just kept increasing. Out of this came the Network of Conscious Judaism and its bookstore. We started these to spread the teachings of Jewish spirituality, psychology, and meditation.

Ety loved her work and her clients, she loved our community and all our friends, and she gave herself to them all. Yet, when we had our first child, Manya, and then Mordechai and Esther, she happily gave up her work in speech therapy to raise them as consciously, as Jewishly, and as lovingly as possible. Our own children blossomed under her "educare." When we moved into a more religious, "yeshiva" community in Santa Clara in 1981, the college-age students as well as some of the rabbi's young children were drawn to our home because of the atmosphere we generated together. People came to drink from Ety's fountain of joy and enjoyment of life. Even in her private life she brought her professional insights on speech and presence. "Use your Shabbos voice," she'd say to me if I was getting too worked up or angry. "Walk your Shabbos walk."

Even when she was diagnosed with breast cancer in 1983, at the age of thirty-eight, in her sixth month of pregnancy with our third child, she faced it straight on. She experimented with

The Soul of the Story

guided imagery, alternative and traditional medicine, Chinese herbal medicine, and macrobiotics. She did everything whole-heartedly, and each contributed toward prolonging the life she so longed for. No matter how difficult or seemingly hopeless it sometimes got, she'd say, "This is going to be the greatest chapter in the book about my recovery!" She would come home after a chemotherapy treatment or a check-up with her oncologist and tell me how *she* helped *him* deal with his burnout. What chutzpah that doctor had. She pays him and *he* gets *her* advice.

Through the guided imagery work, her cancer "spoke" to her and demanded that she become an artist and get out more and relate to nature. So we moved to the countryside of Santa Rosa so we could be surrounded by nature. Aside from the good friends we made there, she became best friends with a eucalyptus tree and a big granite rock that she visited and meditated with every day. When we left Santa Rosa, she said good-bye to them. From the tree, she took some bark, leaves, and pods. Then she went to the rock and put her hands on it for the last time. A chunk of the rock just "broke off" in her hands so she could take a piece of it with her, too.

She spent quality time with the children, sang and danced while she stirred her foul-smelling Chinese herbal healing brews, and painted and explored all sorts of avenues for her art. And if someone looked at her with sad, sympathetic eyes—God save them from her indignant wrath. "Don't look at me like that!" she'd fume, "I'm still very much alive!"

And she fought it off and won the first round.

43

My Honeymoon with Reb Gedaliah

While Ety and I were in Israel on our honeymoon in 1977, I went to see Reb Gedaliah Kenig. Whenever I was with him, my heart beat differently. It was a combination of anticipation, fear, hope, and excitement. (It felt a little like seeing my bride.) Remembering the story of the Hasid who learned from everything the *tzaddik* did, even how he tied his shoelaces, I asked Reb Gedaliah whether I could be around him more, maybe even see him every day (I was too embarrassed to say that I just wanted to follow him around to see how he did everything).

He looked at me, smiling very kindly, and said, "So come tomorrow."

"When?"

He looked at his watch and said, "Like now."

I asked, "You mean I can come tomorrow at this time?"

He nodded very matter-of-factly. "Yes, come every day at this time."

The next day, Reb Gedaliah and I began learning from a book that was a collection of teachings of Rebbe Nachman—*Likutei Aytzot*, later translated into English as *Advice*.

Reb Gedaliah learned with me about Reb Nachman's teaching that you could come to know God only through *emunah*, or faith, because faith—the knowing of the heart—was a much higher state of knowing, of consciousness, than the knowing of the intellect. Reb Nachman taught that you should beware of someone who can prove to you that God exists. "If he can prove that God exists," Rebbe Nachman warned, "he can also prove that God doesn't exist!"

When we believe something, it means that based on what we already know, we believe a certain thing to be true. If someone comes with new information to the contrary, we now believe the opposite. True faith is beyond the intellect. It is a deep intuitive Soul-knowing.

That time every day with Reb Gedaliah was so special. We learned our text, which was a pretext to go into just about anything. I got him to sing *niggunim* (Hasidic melodies). And I got to see him interact with his children and grandchildren. I saw the consistency of his presence, his patience, and his love.

Having my mornings with Reb Gedaliah and the rest of the days with my wife was quite a honeymoon.

44

REB SHLOMO:
Facts and Miracles

Years later, when I was teaching in the Bay Area, Shlomo was coming to town. A student of mine, a doctor, asked whether Shlomo would give a short lunchtime talk to the staff at his hospital. Here was a room full of men and women in white coats, and loudspeakers were constantly paging doctors' names or requesting help or equipment. The staff talked to each other, ate from their lunch bags, and gave half-hearted attention to their guest speaker. And here was Shlomo in slacks, white shirt, vest, and beard, and a *kipa* on his head.

The staff was probably speculating about what someone like Shlomo could possible say to them. Finally, he said, "You know, my sweetest friends, you and I, we come from very different worlds."

Everyone laughed at the obvious observation: Boy, are we different. You're a rabbi and we're secular doctors. Totally different worlds.

But Shlomo had something else in mind. "We come from totally different worlds, because you live in the world of facts and statistics, but I live in the world of miracles!"

The room was so quiet you needed a stethoscope to hear anyone's breath. He had, in fact, taken their breath away. In one sentence, he had touched on what every doctor hardly dares wish he or she could do. Who doesn't want to perform miracles to save lives and cure people suffering from major life-threatening diseases? And many doctors might wish they could pray, but they lacked the faith or the courage to do it. To be a scientist in the face of the unknown, in the face of life and death, was to be a slave to the world of facts and statistics. Who could admit that he only hoped he *could* wish for miracles?

He told Hasidic stories about healing, and about rebbes who healed. He talked about the power of prayer and faith, and that ultimately, everything was in God's hands. The possibilities he presented were deeply healing for these health professionals, many of whom were suffering from burnout and helplessness.

For the rest of his deeply touching talk, Shlomo had their undivided attention. What a skill he had to find the right language, image, and metaphor. What a genius he had for opening lines and opening hearts.

45

No Ordinary Ordination

Transpersonal psychology provided me with the bridge from East to West. It gave me an identity and a community of friends and colleagues; there was a sense of family, of belonging. I felt at home. And now that I was married, I was really at home. And that Jewish home, together with my studies and travels to Israel and continuing contact with my growing number of rebbes and teachers, was building and strengthening my Jewish connection and identity. But the professional pursuits within the transpersonal world were taking the lead for the time being. I still thought I was on a wandering track that was taking me toward being a psychologist and teaching psychology. The role of rabbi had not yet registered. My father's influence and my earlier professional expectations still held sway.

So the move from Southern to Northern California, from helping establish the first undergraduate transpersonal psychology program at Johnston College to helping found the first doctoral program at the Institute of Transpersonal Psychology (ITP) and becoming associate director and professor there, was a transpersonal identity move. That it led me to my wife and establishing my Jewish home still didn't change my personal direction.

But the more I spoke at national and international psychology conferences, and the more I taught at ITP, the more people asked whether I was a rabbi. I was very happy pioneering in transpersonal education and weaving Jewish mystical teachings into it. I had no desire to become a congregational rabbi, or an expert in halacha, Jewish law. It's true, in America, if you had a beard and wore a *kipa,* most people assumed that you were a rabbi. But I wasn't.

I asked Reb Shlomo what he thought about this. He felt that with the amount of public exposure I had, and since I was teaching a lot of Jewish content, maybe it would be worth studying more Jewish law, texts, and commentary on Torah, and actually becoming a rabbi. He knew I wasn't going to be a *posek,* an interpreter of Jewish law. Rather, I would represent and communicate a dimension of Jewish heart and spirituality that was rarely seen in the worlds I moved in. We didn't talk about a time frame. I wasn't looking for a job where the title was essential, and I was already working "full-time" in transpersonal psychology. He gave me a list of subjects he wanted me to study within Talmud, *Shulchan Aruch* (the Code of Jewish Law), and Torah and commentary. I studied with various teachers, read a lot on my own, and wrote papers for him almost every week. Whenever we got together, he would ask questions to check my progress.

ITP was still small enough, and the salary low enough, that I could call it a half-time job. So while Ety worked full-time at the college, I used the other half of my time to pursue my rabbinical studies.

The next time I was in Israel, I asked Reb Gedaliah whether he would be one of the rabbis to grant me my title of rabbi, to give me *smicha.* Today, most people get their rabbinical title from a yeshiva or an educational institution. But traditionally, regardless of where you studied, the ordination came from one or more rabbis who were passing down the "live transmission" to their student. There are rabbis who are "Jewish lawyers," experts in the incredible depth and detail of Jewish law. And there are rabbis who are more teachers in specific areas of study. I didn't want to be a lawyer/rabbi; I wanted to be a spiritual teacher/rabbi. I approached Reb Gedaliah very timidly, knowing that he was aware of how little I knew; I was a little afraid of his rejection or his dismissal.

He looked at me, smiled sweetly and sadly. "I can't give you *smicha*," he said, shaking his head, "because.... "

I anticipated what he was going to say. "I understand." I said, "You don't have to explain.... "

He cut me off. "No, *you* don't understand. I can't give you *smicha* because *I* don't have it myself!" Apparently, with all his learning and knowledge, he had never sought official recognition!

A couple of years later, on a trip to the West Coast, Shlomo said, "Dovidel, it's time to knock off your *smicha*."

"But Shlomo, there's so much more I need to learn."

"I'm not worried, *brother*," he said, "I know you'll be learning for the rest of your life. But now is the time for your *smicha*."

That evening, Shlomo gathered the Carlebach *hevre* (community) together and created a ceremony with a lot of teachings and singing. "Since the time of the Romans," he said, "*smicha*, the direct transmission of student receiving from teacher, had been interrupted. So now we all have to put our hands on Dovidel and reconnect to that transmission." It was deeply empowering. That was part of Shlomo's gift, to re-create ceremonies that most people today are just going through the motions with, whether it's a wedding or an ordination. Slowly, I began to use the title in the teaching that I was doing. And everything was fine.

Then, around 1982, an old friend who had become more ultra-Orthodox, challenged me about using my title where it might actually lead people away from Judaism. "How can you use your title of rabbi when you go to some of those places? What if they think it's kosher, because they see your title 'rabbi'? You can't do that!"

Well, by now we were living in Santa Clara, California, in a small community connected with Kerem Yeshiva, which was a satellite campus of one of the most prestigious ultra-Orthodox yeshivas—Ner Yisrael, based in Baltimore. It just happened that one of the highest rabbinical authorities, Rabbi Yaakov Yitzchok Ruderman, the head of Ner Yisrael, was in town. In the Jewish legal hierarchy, he was the equivalent of a Supreme Court judge. His decisions were as high as you could go. I went to see him in the middle of the week. He was very old and his eyeglasses were as thick as Coke bottles.

I explained that my *smicha* was from Rabbi Shlomo Carlebach and told him what I had learned, and more importantly, how I was using the title and the places I was going. I told him that someone had challenged me about using the title of rabbi.

Asking very precise, detailed questions, he conducted a serious cross-examination. He wanted to know where I went and what I taught and what I did. He wanted to know my motivations. He wanted to be sure that I wasn't trying to convert people, but just represent Judaism. He then told me he needed three days to think about it. Then he would give me his answer.

After the evening prayers that Friday night, we all got in line to say "Good Shabbos" to the rabbis at the yeshiva. When I got to Rabbi Ruderman, he squinted at me through his thick glasses and said, "Didn't we talk the other day about your *smicha* and using your title of rabbi?"

"Yes we did," I responded, with a slight tremble.

"One hundred percent! You go out into the world and you use your title of rabbi."

That was it! It was almost more dramatic than the original *smicha* from Shlomo, and it was a tremendous validation of Shlomo and for me and my work. It also opened my eyes to the depth and vision and openness of people like Rav Ruderman, a man deeply rooted in the ultra-Orthodox tradition who, despite his poor physical eyesight, was able to see so clearly and make such liberal and creative decisions.

46

JACK SHWARZ:
Beyond Our Physical Bodies

As a young man in Holland, Jack Shwarz and his family were tortured by the Nazis for helping Jews. Jack discovered that he could control his pain and instantly heal himself from any wounds the Germans inflicted. After the war, he began working in the sideshow of a circus, lying on a bed of nails with a heavy boulder on top of him pushing his body further onto the nails. Then he would stand up, showing people his back. As they looked, he would stop the bleeding and heal the wounds.

The United States Army, Navy, and Air Force studied, tested, researched, and experimented on Jack, hooking him up to biological measuring and monitoring devices for heart rate, brain wave, nerve impulse, and so on. They filmed him and the monitors as he pushed a bicycle spoke through his upper arm. Nothing registered, nothing showed. They were stumped.

"Maybe you're a zombie, or just can't feel anything," they suggested.

"Oh! Would you like to see my body reacting?" he asked. He released some inner control, and his arm started bleeding and all the monitors started going crazy, recording the trauma to all systems in the body.

"Now," he said, "I'll bring everything back to normal." And the monitors returned to normal, and the wounds healed and disappeared.

In another experiment, he was put into a sealed room with very limited oxygen and remained there for days, far longer than any ordinary human could. The monitors registered that all of his bodily functions had slowed down and he was consuming very little air. He had no food or water all that time, and continued to have normal bowel movements. It was like he was eating full meals from the atmosphere. No one knew what to make of this.

Jack realized that this was a special gift, and he began to discover he had other psychic sensitivities as well. He learned as much as he could about these abilities and tried to teach them to others. He always said he didn't think he was unique or had special powers. He was sure that anyone could achieve what he had. He was just here to show people what was possible.

Aside from his tremendous control of his "involuntary" nervous system, Jack became an excellent psychic. He saw auras around people. To him, these looked like the rings of a tree. He would see something and kind of squint as he counted the rings to determine when a particular event had happened in your life. Then he'd say, "It looks like in 1957, something happened that affected your.... " And he would proceed to check you out further.

Whereas some psychics would tell you what was wrong with you, Jack had a gift to put everything in the most positive framework. If you had a weakness, he would tell you how to develop your strengths, and then he'd talk about uplifting and transforming the weakness itself. Whatever the problem, he would recommend vitamins, minerals, or homeopathic remedies that would help balance things.

I had many meetings and readings with Jack. He was always dressed immaculately in a turtleneck and sports jacket. His beard was neatly trimmed. He was a true gentleman.

When I first met Jack, he said he wanted to tune into Sri Pad, my teacher from India, but for some reason he couldn't psychically "find" him. This was before computers and the Internet, but it was like he couldn't find him on the world wide *psychic* web. He asked me to visualize him in my mind. Then he got a very strong impression of him and said, "No wonder I couldn't locate him. Most gurus are drawing people to them and holding onto them; but your teacher is always pushing people away, making them stand up on their own two feet!"

Once when I went to see him with my wife, he said, "Mazel tov!" then proceeded to give a reading on our first child. This was before Ety was even showing.

A couple of years later, we went to see him again. This time Jack didn't notice that she was pregnant. "Jack! Didn't you see that she's pregnant?"

He took a deeper look and said, "The aura of this child is so similar to the mother that they overlapped completely and I didn't see any separate presence."

I had many conversations and sessions with Jack, but I particularly remember him saying, "If someone asks you to do something that you don't think you can do—*do it*! The reason he is asking *you,* and not someone else, is because he, or God, knows that you *can* do it. Don't just listen to yourself. Listen to what the universe is asking of you."

I've tried to follow his advice and, although I haven't developed such healing abilities, knowing that Jack has them and that they are real has given me the confidence to try to heal my own children. When they were young, I would hold whatever was hurt between both my hands and focus all the energy and life force in me to flow into it, making my hands vibrate rapidly. I would also make an electric buzzing sort of sound, almost like "jjjjjjjjjjjjj." It seemed to really help, and now my children do it to my grandchildren if I'm not there to do it myself. And I try to heal others with my hands and mainly with my prayers, and I believe it makes a difference.

47

SWAMI RADHA:
Bending Over Backwards
for Others

In the late 1970s, Swami Radha came each year to teach a week-long intensive in yoga psychology for students at the Institute of Transpersonal Psychology. She was among the disciples of Swami Sivananda. Hatha yoga, the yoga of postures for physical and mental health, had already come to the West, but Swami Sivananda inspired his students to teach the yoga postures together with the philosophy, in a context of service to God and guru and humanity. Among his most well-known students was Swami Vishnu Devananda, who published the first comprehensive yoga book, *The Complete Illustrated Book of Yoga*. He and Swami Satchitananda each created his own network of yoga centers in many cities around the world, offering classes and teacher-training courses that really made yoga a household word and readily available for anyone seeking to learn it.

Swami Radha was probably the first woman from the West to go to India and become a swami back in the 1950s. But something else made her stand out even more. Once, a follower told her that he had not come to her about a problem he was having because her holy orange robes elevated her so high above the mundane. She was so upset that her "holy" garments were creating such a distance that she began dressing in ordinary Western clothing. Now, minus her sari, she looked like a little old lady with nicely coifed silver-gray hair. But it was still her! Same wisdom, same loving and fearful demanding approach to spiritual accountability and growth.

Yet most of her students left her. It seems they were devoted to her orange sari more than to her remarkable teachings and practices. This was very similar to the Hasidic story of Reb Zusha:

> Zusha walked into a town looking like a vagabond. Only the simple folks paid attention to him and invited him to their homes for Shabbat. When he returned the next time on a horse and wagon, he was recognized as a *tzaddik* (a righteous person) and invited to stay with the town's wealthiest scholar. Reb Zusha sent his horse and wagon there and returned to the house of the simple folks he had stayed with formerly. When the wealthy scholar's servant came to ask why he had sent his wagon to the house but stayed in this hovel, he replied, "When I came the first time my host took me in as I was. I'm still who I am. Since I was now invited by such a scholar, I figured he was really interested in my horse and wagon— so I sent that on to his house."

After donning Western clothes, Swami Radha continued to teach, slowly building up a new community of followers. Where other yoga teachers told you to come with yoga mat, and maybe a tongue scraper and cloth to swallow for cleansing practices, Swami Radha told you to bring a typewriter (no, not to swallow). She wanted you to write your thoughts, associations, meditations, and symbols on every posture that she taught, and every part of the body that she had you focus on. For example, if the focus was on the hand, you might write, "I've got to hand it to you.... I've never been very handy.... He was hoping for a handout.... I can't grasp what you're saying .... I can't quite put my finger on it.... My hands are clean of this.... " And so on.

But what fascinated me the most about the way she taught yoga was her metaphoric use of the postures themselves. When doing stretches, such as arching the back and all the bones of the spine, she would say, "That's pretty good, but can you practice bending over backwards for people in your lives? Can you bend over backwards to help someone—even a stranger—in need?"

And when we did the headstand, with our head on the floor and our feet straight up in the air, she would comment, "That's very good! You can be completely upside down, and still keep your balance, and even keep your breath deep and relaxed. And you can even keep your eyes open while you're doing it. But can you be in a situation with people who stand totally opposite to what you believe in? Can you keep your balance, and keep your breathing deep and relaxed? Can you keep your eyes open? Only then will you have mastered the headstand."

She lived and practiced with a congruency that was her best teaching. She taught by her own example. For Swami Radha, there was no separation between the postures in yoga and our postures and positions in the rest of our lives.

For me, this resonated so much with Rebbe Nachman's various practices for meditating on parts of the body: I need my legs to walk to the house of study and prayer, to stand before God in prayer, and to run and do a mitzvah, a good deed for someone. But what if I'm using my legs to go where no good is accomplished or, God forbid, where actual negative actions are generated? What right, then, do I have to walk on the ground without thanking God? Just because I stood before God this morning doesn't excuse me from standing before God now, in the form of this person I'm interacting with.

If there had been a point in my life where I considered pursuing my strong connection to India, or perhaps becoming a swami, Swami Radha provided a most special model for me. The balance and blend of the yoga and the psychological disciplines of the East and the West were very much in tune with so much of my life and beliefs. I went to her community in Canada to teach, and I was very impressed with how her students were learning to walk that real walk. She was a remarkable teacher.

Shortly after I got married and decided to become a rabbi, I got a package from her filled with cloth. It wasn't her orange robes. It was her white lace and embroidered fancy tablecloths and napkins that she still had from her family in Austria.

"I really don't need these fancy tablecloths for my practice," she wrote in a note. "But in your religious life, you will have much use for this on your Shabbat and holiday table. With blessings, Swami Radha."

48

KENNETT ROSHI: Beaten to Enlightenment

While Swami Radha was petite in her silver-gray coif and her white double-knit suitpants, Kennett Roshi was large and round like the Buddha. Her head was shaved bald, and she wore traditional black-and-brown Zen robes.

Kennett Roshi had also broken through a major glass ceiling in the conservative post–World War II Japanese Zen world. A woman in the monastery? Studying and practicing being a monk, maybe even a Zen master? And not only a woman, but a woman from England—which had fought Japan during the war.

According to her own account, she said that the other Zen monks never missed an opportunity to ambush her and beat her soundly. Though they thought that would discourage her from pursuing her goal, they literally beat her into enlightenment.

Now many years later she was a Zen master. Distinguishing her from so many other spiritual teachers was her commitment to helping everyone, regardless of his or her path. She wanted everyone to develop as fully as he or she could. Like the bodhisattva, she had vowed to help everyone achieve enlightenment.

Amid many hours of meditation and teachings that she was giving at the Institute for Transpersonal Psychology, she had us play a game that had been played for centuries in Zen monasteries. It was a kind of "karmic" Chutes and Ladders, with several concentric circles, each representing a "higher" level of awareness. These circles included various situations and opportunities, depending on the fateful throw of the dice, to pick cards that either rewarded you with extra "good karma" points, or sent you up to the next higher level or to a lower level. Everything was filled with learning and practices of wisdom, compassion, and contemplation. Many places we landed on led to a full teaching about the situation at hand and the compassionate response. There was a window with various layers covering it that came with the board, and as you went up to higher levels of consciousness, the layers were removed, indicating that your advance brought more light into the world for everyone; as you slid back down, the layers were reapplied, returning the world to darkness. Some of the advances were really in your control, and much was also up to fortune.

There was one other factor. Beyond the framework of the game, with its ups and downs, stood the Zen teachers. They watched how you took your ups and downs, and the ups and downs of others in the game. Were you too gleeful at your own good fortune or at someone else's bad fortune? Were you too despondent at you own loss or at someone else's gain? The observing teachers might give you extra "good karma" cards or take away some of what you had accumulated.

We could play this remarkable teaching tool for hours. It was just like life. But the game was only as good as the "game master," and Kennett Roshi was the best. Her perceptions of subtle shifts of consciousness or unconsciousness, rising and sinking like the waves of the ocean, were very penetrating. She could be very strict and demanding, yet she had the most wicked (and, I guess, British) sense of humor. And despite her attire and her baldness, she was personable and approachable, caring and compassionate.

Perhaps it goes with being a Zen master, but Kennett Roshi was delightfully mischievous. She could teach or do something with such a gleam in her eye. At the same time, she could be very tough and demanding with students! But her humor was very special.

One time, she said, "I want to teach you one of the most important mantras. I teach it to all my advanced students who are on the way to becoming Zen teachers themselves."

We all sat up extra attentively.

"Would you like to learn it?" she asked.

We all nodded enthusiastically.

"Then repeat after me: 'I ... could ... be ... wrong.' This can be said in many different variations: 'I *could* be wrong.' Or 'I could be *wrong*.' Or '*I* could be wrong.' Or '*I* could be *wrong*?' Practice this often. You can't be a good and true teacher without knowing it well."

In a world of "all-knowing" and "perfected" masters, this was so refreshing and realistic. I continue to quote her teaching, and I still try to practice it. It rates very high on my top-ten mantra list, along with "I'm sorry. I made a mistake. Please forgive me." I have often done workshops for teachers and taught them a variation of "I could be wrong," which is, "I don't know." (And all the ways to emphasize its three words.) "That's a very good question. I'm going to have to do some research of my own or ask one of *my* teachers. Thank you."

Here again was a teacher from yet another tradition who practiced it and lived it right into everyday life, far beyond the limits of the tradition itself.

49

CARL ROGERS: Manipulative?

The conference of the Association of Humanistic Psychology was dedicated to humanistic values in politics, and I had been asked to sing a song or two between some of the speakers. I came on stage just as Carl Rogers was finishing his talk on how to inject his philosophy of unconditional positive regard into politics.

I had never met Carl, but he was still on stage as I began settling in. Turning to him, I said, "I'm so glad to be here with you at this particular conference. For a long time, I've wanted to say to you that I think you're one of the most manipulative people I know."

The audience gasped. I didn't think my life was in danger. After all, the room was filled with "humanistic" people. But I quickly added, "Please let me explain what I mean. From my years in India, spirituality, and transpersonal psychology, I've come to appreciate how hard it is to really see a person with unconditional positive regard, to truly see someone without the judgmental filters that normally distort our perception. From the teachers I have been blessed to be with, I have come to understand that looking at people with such love and compassion means *not* seeing or accepting them as they are. *It means seeing them as they could be!* You see them in their full potential. You see their soul and its vision and purpose. Love isn't accepting people as they are. Love is seeing people as they could be, as their soul intended them to be.

"When you look at people like that, with unconditional positive regard, and they feel themselves really being seen, perhaps for the first time in their life, they have *no choice* but to change, to come closer to their soul's purpose.

"And that's manipulation. But it's one of the highest services you can do to another human being. Thank you."

From the look he gave me, it was clear that he knew, deeply, what I meant.

Many people thought that Carl Rogers's therapy was simply listening to people, nodding your head wisely, saying "Uh-huh," and reflecting back what they just said. But real healing therapy isn't just hearing someone's pain and empathizing with it. What someone does might cause himself outer pain and suffering, but the real pain is the soul's pain from knowing what could have been and what you are truly capable of doing. This is the pain of the missed opportunity. It's the pain someone else (or your own soul) feels when seeing you do something that's off. Seeing the pain that someone else feels for you can help you change enormously.

A woman once told me that she stole some comic books when she was a child. Very excited, she showed her best friend what she had done. To her surprise, her friend cried. And she was so moved by her friend's regret over her actions that she returned the comic books and never stole again.

Guilt on the ego level comes from knowing you did something wrong and feeling bad about it. Guilt on the soul level is spiritual pain: it's your soul knowing you could do so much better.

It's like Shlomo's teaching about the vow each soul makes before being born. Throughout our lives, we are either moving closer to that soul purpose or farther away from it. Our soul feels when we come closer. And those who can see with unconditional positive regard see it and help us get there.

50

Ram Dass:
Memorable and
Memorial Meetings

In the late 1970s, friends of my wife Ety invited us to a going-away party. They were taking a sabbatical from his research on chimpanzee intelligence at Stanford University. At their house, I met another couple, and, instead of being with our friends who were going away, I spent the whole evening talking with them. They were fascinated to meet an Orthodox Jew who had been to India and met so many gurus. I discovered they were very close with Ram Dass.

Less than a week later, Ety and I were at the market and by chance glanced at the front page of the local newspaper. A Stanford professor of mathematics had been murdered by one of his students. His picture was on the front page.

"Isn't that the man you were talking to the other night at the party?"

I took a closer look, and we read the name under the picture: Karel deLeeuw. It was definitely him. We had just met and now he was murdered!

Though we hardly knew each other, I called his wife, Sita, now so suddenly a widow, and asked whether there was anything I could do as a new friend or maybe, more importantly, as a rabbi. It turned out that my call meant a lot to her. She never thought that there could be anything meaningful from Judaism to help her cope with this tragedy. She asked whether

I would officiate at the memorial service for her husband, and I immediately agreed.

Soon she called back. "Could I ask a big favor?"

"Of course! What is it?"

"Do you remember we told you how close we were with Ram Dass? Well, I just spoke with him and he offered to do something at the memorial. Is that okay? Will that work with whatever Jewish prayers you were going to do?"

I assured her it would be okay, telling her that I had a good relationship with him after we had reconnected a few years earlier in Los Angeles. He had been giving an evening *satsang* of chanting and teaching, and I had been hungry for a little taste of India. In the middle of his teachings, he told about being in Vrindavan and feeling a little down when two American sadhus knocked on his door, bringing some "food for the soul" and lifting his spirits. "There I was," I told Sita, "sitting in the audience while he told people about the time I brought him *prasad* from Sri Pad!"

After his talk that night, I went up to him and said, "I'm the sadhu who brought you the *prasad*!" Our personal association had begun. He spoke to my students at Johnston College, and a few years later, he spoke to our PhD students at ITP. It was so meaningful for our students to hear from him personally and follow his journey from traditional psychology to spirituality. His discoveries in that process were very important for them.

So Ram Dass and I did the memorial ceremony together. There was room for both traditions—Hinduism and Judaism— and at the end, Ram Dass said to me, "I like the way you *Jewish*."

And I liked being able to "Jewish" as an Orthodox rabbi, in such a wide range of spiritual settings. It was very gratifying to have developed a formula for Jewish spirituality that worked so harmoniously with people like Ram Dass. It felt good to be as flexible and creative as possible in order to serve people in some very unusual circumstances.

Several years went by with little contact with Ram Dass. And when I moved to Israel in 1985, it was even harder to stay in touch.

Then, around 1992, I was on a lecture/concert tour in Los Angeles when I heard that Ram Dass was also in town giving a talk. To my delight, it was on an evening that I was free. Not only that, but he was giving a talk on his reflections on Judaism! It turned out that it was the first memorial lecture to commemorate the death of Gerald Goldfarb, who had been murdered a year previously in a drive-by shooting. I called for tickets and was told it was sold out. I was very disappointed. Luckily, a friend gave me the phone number of Gerald's widow, Lilly, who had organized the event, and I gave her a call.

"I just happened to be in town from Israel on a lecture tour and found out that Ram Dass is giving a talk on Judaism. It's the one evening I have open. Is there any way to get a seat?"

"There's not a seat available in the whole hall," she said, "but there is a seat for you on stage."

"What?" I asked in surprise.

"When Gerald was murdered, there were two things that kept me going: Ram Dass's teachings and your singing. I never dreamed that I could have the two of you together for this memorial. But if you'd open the evening with some songs before he speaks, it would mean so much to me."

So there I was on stage, sitting next to my old friend Ram Dass and opening the event with a number of songs. His talk covered his fairly observant upbringing until the age of six or so, when his family became more conservative. He talked about his perception of Jewish teachings after his awakenings from LSD and Eastern meditation. It was a very interesting perspective.

Afterward I said to him, "We really can't go on meeting like this."

"Like this?" he asked.

I said, "Do you remember the last time we were together?"

"No, when was it?"

"At the memorial for another murder victim: Karel deLeeuw. Let's try to get together more often, without horrible things like this bringing us together."

He agreed.

Then I said, "Now that you've given a talk on Judaism, maybe it's time for us to meet next in Israel. Please come, I'll personally show you the country—its archeological past and its mystical present and presence. I'll arrange for you to give some teachings there as well."

"I'll let you know the next time I have a teaching in Europe," he said, "and I'll come to Israel then."

And it was agreed. And it happened.

But that's another story.

51

SWAMI VISHNU DEVANANDA: Unity in Diversity

In 1978, I was invited to be a guest speaker at Swami Vishnu Devananda's yoga retreat center in the Bahamas. One of the early masters of hatha yoga to come to America, he wrote *The Complete Illustrated Book of Yoga*, the first comprehensive yoga book. He opened centers around the world where people could learn yoga and attend workshops in holistic health, environment, music and the arts, and more. Located in the Bahamas, Montreal, India, and Europe, they were a wonderful way to attract people.

Once again, I was delighted to see that identifying so strongly with Judaism and becoming an Orthodox rabbi had not cut me off from the other traditions. I was entering into a dialogue with a range of teachers, each coming from the heart of a specific religion, but also concerned with our commonality.

Each day, a different teacher would speak to the whole group. Swami Vishnu would sit on stage, to the side, and often interject into the middle of someone's talk his own insights or show the parallel to yoga teachings.

While I was on stage singing and teaching about Jewish mysticism and meditation, Swami Vishnu chimed in, "Oh, Rabbi, this is just like we teach in yoga philosophy. You see, we really are all one, and all the teachings are here in yoga!"

I didn't know the rules of the game. Apparently, it was okay for him to interrupt his guest speakers, but it wasn't okay for me to interrupt him. I plunged ahead anyway.

"No Swamiji, we're not all one. We're all different. We are all part of one greater whole, but that whole depends on each part fulfilling its separate function: unity in diversity. In Kabbalah, we learn that the human body is a metaphor for the world. My body is whole and healthy *because* each separate organ and system is doing its task in harmony with all the others. But if my liver could convince the other organs that being a liver is really where it's at and convinced them all to be livers, I'd be one big liver! And I'd be dead! I am whole and healthy because each part is playing its distinctive role.

"Each religion, each people, each culture is like an organ in the body of humankind. But for all humanity to be truly whole and harmonious, each part must fulfill its mission while recognizing the essential importance of all the others. Each people is chosen to be the organ that it is, with its particular purpose, for the good of the whole world. Today, we suffer a lot from religions that say, '*This* is the only way, and everyone must be like us and accept our way.' We must accept and nurture our differences for the good of the whole."

I don't think the swami and I were in disagreement. It was more a question of semantics. But when it comes to that, you could say that I'm somewhat anti-*semantic*.

One of the remarkable things that I most admire about Swami Vishnu Devananda was that, as much as he was the inspirational force of all his organization's activities, he had built it in such a way that it would carry on his vision after he died. He created the "healthy organs" that would sustain his vision. It is quite rare among spiritual teachers to be so future-oriented. He divided the retreat and city centers among his top student swamis and had them rotate as guest teachers in each other's centers. He established meetings and decision-making processes that could be maintained by phone, e-mail, and Internet and that could be done while each was in his or her different and distant part of the world.

Swami Vishnu did wonderful work by bringing such a variety of teachers together for the conference-retreats, and in such an intimate atmosphere: Turkish Sufis, Native Americans, Tibetan monks, classic musicians and dancers from India and other countries, Christian priests and ministers, rabbis, healers of many persuasions, scholars and experts on every imaginable subject—from the environment to aliens—and maybe even a couple of aliens themselves. Though Swami Vishnu passed away in 1993, these dialogues are still going on at his centers, and I'm very pleased to still be part of that greater whole.

When Edith Sullwold, a Jungian, was a guest teacher at the Institute of Transpersonal Psychology, one of our students talked about being One with everyone. Edith said that if we explore the language of no boundaries and all being one in the medical journals, we will find it is the description of cancer. There are no distinctions, no boundaries, no borders—all is one—but it's cancer, and the system will die from that oneness.

52

REB GEDALIAH:
The Institute of
Transpersonal Psychology

Reb Gedaliah Kenig was coming to America. It was 1979, and this was a rare opportunity. Though I had brought many teachers—famous and relatively unknown—to meet with students at the Institute of Transpersonal Psychology in the past, this seemed different. Reb Gedaliah wasn't a public figure. He wasn't really involved with much of the Jewish world, let alone the non-Jewish world. He didn't "do" workshops or retreats. He hadn't written any popular books on spirituality. He didn't have an organization around him. He usually just sat quietly in his home or in the Breslov yeshiva, learning and teaching. He was very humble and unassuming.

Now he was leaving Israel, traveling to gain support for his project to build a Breslov community in Sefat. He was only planning to go to New York, but I convinced him to come to California to teach and meet some people in the world of transpersonal psychology and spirituality.

For weeks in advance, I helped my PhD students at the Institute prepare for Reb Gedaliah's visit. In particular, we learned about Rebbe Nachman and his story of the Lost Princess. In this story, Rebbe Nachman tells of a king who loves his daughter very much. But after he got angry at her once, she disappeared. The very long, elaborate story is about the adventures of the king's minister as he searches for her and finds her. But to free her, he must sit a whole year longing for her, and on the last day before coming to get her, he must fast, not eating or drinking anything. Alas! On the last day, after fasting most of the day, he eats a fruit. After failing this test, he's given a second year, requiring only that he not *drink* on the last day. He drinks and again fails his test. This time she is moved to a new, far-away place, and he must go on an even lengthier search for her that takes him beyond all known realms of beings and existence. In the end he finds her again, but the story stops there and we don't know how or when she is freed.

My students and I considered all sorts of interpretations for this story, from Jung to Hasidism. We focused especially on the meditation practices that the story strongly hinted at by telling us that he had to sit for a year yearning for her. We looked at the ideas of the Four Worlds. We explored the parallels between images in the story to aspects of biblical narrative: eating the fruit of the Tree of Knowledge, Noah drinking and getting drunk, the revelation at Mount Sinai, and more. We delved into the story as the process we all must go through while seeking our true inner Soul.

We covered much ground. But still, we were unprepared for Reb Gedaliah's interpretation of the story. He especially focused on the apparently introductory sentences that led to the real essence of Rebbe Nachman's story:

One time he was alone with her on a certain day and he became angry at her. He inadvertently said, "May the Evil One take you away!"

At night, she went to her room. In the morning, no one knew where she was. Her father was very upset, and he went here and there looking for her.

The viceroy realized that the king was very upset. He stood up and asked that the king give him a servant, a horse, and some money for expenses, and he went to search for her. He searched for her very much, for a very long time, until he found her.[7]

After reviewing this passage, Reb Gedaliah said, "The most important thing about the story is...." He paused and we leaned in to take in his every word. "The most important thing about the story is how many years and how much work it takes to fix the damage from just one moment of anger.... The story helps us understand how much work we all have to do to fix ourselves and the world."

He went on at some length and with amazing depth. I was impressed with how this rebbe, immersed in his world of Jewish life, thought, and practice, pulled out the theme most relevant for these doctoral students of psychology. He had shifted the focus from the spiritual and the meditative to the psychological work of dealing with anger and what is required to clean up the mess it always creates.

While in the Bay Area, I arranged for Reb Gedaliah to give one class open to the general public and a second private event in our home for prominent people in the world of psychology and spirituality, along with some potential donors for Reb Gedaliah's Sefat project. The guests included Ram Dass and Claudio Naranjo, a Gestalt psychiatrist and "visionary anthropologist" who guided small groups through spiritual transformation. He also worked with mind-altering substances to facilitate therapeutic breakthroughs. He called these "artificial sanity, a temporary anesthesia of the neurotic Self."

I wanted these spiritual teachers, who were Jewish, to know that our tradition still had valuable teachers. I wanted them to meet someone who was such a deep wellspring of Jewish wisdom and compassion.

That night at my house, Reb Gedaliah, in his usual humble, unassuming way, gave over the teachings of Rebbe Nachman that no matter how far you are into yourself and the material world around you, you can reach beyond your ego to connect to your soul and to God. But at one point, Reb Gedaliah said, "And Rebbe Nachman says that even one who feels so far away from God can come so close...." His translator who was from Brooklyn, said, "And Rebbe Nachman says that even the worst Jew alive can repent, do *teshuvah*, and come back to God...."

My knowledge of Hebrew was good enough to know what Reb Gedaliah was really saying. To my dismay, I realized the translation wasn't into California English; he was translating into *Brooklyn* English. He wasn't translating from the heart, but from the head.

Ram Dass said to me afterward, "It's too bad you had a translator. His presence is so high, I could sit with him forever. It's the message that drives me away. But I'm so glad to know teachers like Reb Gedaliah exist."

I have encountered this problem so often: so many people in the Jewish world express the tradition in ways that leaves its psychological and spiritual dimensions inaccessible to outsiders.

One sweet moment from that evening came when the elderly mother of one of my guests extended her hand to Reb Gedaliah, saying, "Thank you so much."

There was that usually awkward moment between religious men and nonreligious women about shaking hands or hugging. Some have drawn away, saying, "Don't touch!" Others have said politely, "I don't touch women."

Reb Gedaliah gently pulled his hands back, looked at her with such love and respect, and simply said, "I only touch my wife." It seemed like she almost melted from such a gracious and loving response.

For me, watching the way he handled that interaction between religious and nonreligious worlds was like watching how he tied his shoelaces.

53

A Native American
Rosh HaShanah

In 1981, I got a phone call inviting me to a gathering of teachers from many spiritual traditions. The conference had been called by Mad Bear, a prominent Indian medicine man from the Northeast.

The conference coordinator explained that for years the United States government had assisted Indians by building drug, alcohol, and family rehabilitation facilities. But, he said, the government didn't understand that these problems were only symptoms of a much greater problem:

"You see," he said, *"the moral fiber of the planet is deteriorating.* Knowledge of spiritual realities and their accompanying values is being lost. The way of living those values in our day-to-day life of ritual and ceremony and family and life cycle is disappearing. Consciously or unconsciously, our people are so sensitive to this loss. It causes tremendous pain. Drugs and alcohol are an ineffective means to dull the pain and suffering.

"We don't need more rehab programs! We need to heal the moral fiber of the planet. We need to revive our people's traditional teachings and practices that have been denied us for so long by Western culture."

He explained that the "summit," as it was called, was originally planned exclusively for Native American teachers and leaders, but they decided to expand it to teachers and elders of all traditions. They were asking me to be a representative of the Jewish people. I was very touched to be included.

"So when is this gathering going to take place?" I asked.

"We picked the most auspicious month of the year, and the holiest day of that moon cycle."

The date he gave me was the exact time of Rosh HaShanah—the New Year!

"That is the holiest of months for the Jewish people, too," I said, "and the holiest day of that month. That day coincides with the creation of the world. But unfortunately I can't attend because we have our own ceremonies and rituals for those two days."

A few minutes after I'd regretfully declined, he called back saying that they decided to hold a preconference meeting for the Native American teachers on their holy time and during Rosh HaShanah. The official summit would start the next day. This way, I could attend. Their accommodation and, more so, their respect for the holy days of others deeply impressed me. I could remember several earlier New Age and "spiritual" gatherings that did not recognize or accommodate the Sabbath or other Jewish religious holy days. This oversight especially excluded Orthodox Jews from participating.

This was also in contrast to conferences that claimed to be for all traditions but used expressions like "Christ Consciousness." When I suggested that they use a term like "Universal Consciousness" that would truly include non-Christian-based religions, I was told, "You Jews are holding up the consciousness of the planet." I knew they meant "blocking" the consciousness, but I couldn't help thinking that maybe we really were helping to "hold up," *to support,* the consciousness of the planet, and keep it from falling. I knew that this summit organized by Native Americans would be different.

Since the event was being held at a Native American holy place just outside Kansas City, I made plans to celebrate Rosh HaShanah with a small Orthodox community in Kansas City. The conference coordinators asked when the holy day would be over so they could pick me up. I told them that I didn't know the exact time because that's determined by the appearance of the first three stars in the evening sky. There was a lot of excitement on their end because we both measured time with the moon and the stars.

At the sight of three stars, they picked me up and took me to the summit. They had lit a huge bonfire, and asked me to share something about the ritual of Rosh HaShanah.

Standing before the fire, before all the people who had gathered, I said a few words about how Rosh HaShanah is the time that Jews acknowledge the Creator, from whom comes the purpose and vision for the whole world, and for all of life. During Rosh HaShanah, each Jew renews his or her soul's individual vision and purpose in relation to God's all-inclusive vision and purpose. Then I pulled out my shofar, my ram's horn, and sounded the "call" of Rosh HaShanah. Again, we were bonded by a practice that tied us together with nature and with God.

This was immediately followed by a Native American "Thanksgiving" ceremony. Calling out to the Earth, they gave thanks to the Earth that we could stand and walk upon it, and build from its mud and stones, and that we could live on it and plant food on it. And they thanked the Earth for following the Will of the Creator.

They gave thanks to the Heavens for the Sun and the Moon and the clouds without which we could not live and plants could not grow. And they gave thanks to the Heavens for following the Will of the Creator.

Then they gave thanks for the Water that helps all plants and trees grow, and provides us with water to drink and bathe in, and provides a home for the fish. And they thanked the Water for following the Will of the Creator.

They gave thanks to all the Plant life, from tiny herbs to giant trees, for their healing medicines, their roots, fruits, and barks; for food, color, shelter, and so much more. And they thanked the Plant world for following the Will of the Creator.

They gave thanks to all Animals for their milk, their wool, their meat, and their furs, skins, and bones. They thanked their horses for riding and carrying. And they thanked the Animal world for following the Will of the Creator.

I'm sure I haven't done justice to all the details of their ceremony, but two important things stood out. With all parts of creation, they focused their ultimate thanks for following the

Will of the Creator. The overall existence of the Creator and the Will of that Creator was very strong and constantly present. The second remarkable thing was that it did not thank the human realm of creation. Rather, the ceremony mentioned repeatedly how humans benefited from all the rest of creation. And humanity wasn't thanked for following the Will of the Creator. This suggested that we are the exception to all of creation, that we *don't* follow the Will of the Creator, that we are not in harmony with creation and the Creator.

Coming on the heels of Rosh HaShanah, when Jews are judged for how far we have wandered from *our* vision and purpose in relation to *God's* vision and purpose, this was, indeed, a most auspicious month for me.

Particularly powerful was a sweat lodge ceremony conducted by Phillip Deere, an Oglala Sioux medicine man. We were bent over in the small, dark, womblike space, the bent branches of the lodge similar to the curved ribs of our mothers who had brought us into the world. The lodge was filled with the herbal steam from the water that was poured over hot stones in the center of the lodge. As we sat, prayers were offered in many languages and from many traditions.

The conference was very special. People spoke from such a place of caring for all people and all life. There was a real understanding that all our paths contained the wisdom that could heal the planet and steer humanity away from moral disintegration. Most politicians, we knew, didn't understand the problems of society from this spiritual perspective. So they only proposed superficial solutions. Our job was to make a statement from a higher ground. We wrote a declaration that was sent around to various government agencies and to Congress. Though it came from our hearts, it was hard to reach their ears.

54

SHLOMO, ZALMAN, AND ME:
Jewish and Transpersonal
in India

The Association of Transpersonal Psychology was now planning its next international conference, to be held in Bombay,
India. They had invited Mother Teresa, Swami Muktananda, a
representative of the Dalai Lama, and others.

I called the organizers and asked why there were only religious teachers from the East. After all, I pointed out, we are a
Western psychological association. Where are the representatives of other faiths? Even the Christian representatives were
natives of India or they had lived there a long time. Where
were the Jews, the Muslims, the Native Americans, and so
many others? It was clear that I was primarily concerned
about Jewish representation, not just because of my own lean-
ings, but also because transpersonal psychology included a
high percentage of Jews.

The organizers explained that they didn't know who the out-
standing spiritual teachers in the Jewish world were, or how to
contact them. I mentioned that I was a rabbi and a founding
member of the association and that maybe I could help out. I
mentioned the Lubavitcher Rebbe, the spiritual head of the
Chabad movement. I also mentioned an internationally
respected rebbe, Rabbi Adin Steinsaltz, who had written many
books on Hasidism and supervised the translation of the
Talmud into Hebrew, and Rabbi Aryeh Kaplan, a great translator and interpreter of Hasidic and kabbalistic texts and con-

cepts. I didn't really think that these people would come to a conference like this, so I also suggested Shlomo Carlebach, Zalman Schachter, and myself. After more convincing, they made time for us on the program. And so the three of us made our way to Bombay.

We were scheduled for a Wednesday evening. There had been many workshops, panels, and keynote speeches during the proceeding days. The evening events were in a theater with a rotating stage. The acoustics were very good. During the previous events, with various gurus and spiritual teachers, people had sat quietly and meditatively. Now we came on stage, and Shlomo took the microphone and said, "My sweetest friends, Zalman and Dovidel and I—we are so disgustingly Jewish.... "

I nearly *plotzed*, thinking, "Shlomo, what are you doing? Do you know who you are talking to?" I just couldn't believe what he was saying.

Then he continued, "But we are intoxicated by the holiness of this beautiful country and by all these beautiful people.... "

After some singing, Zalman led everyone in a beautiful "Universal Mass" through the Four Worlds, bringing all the traditions into focus. Soon we were singing again and, for the first time at the conference, everyone got up and physically reached out beyond themselves, holding hands and dancing and dancing and dancing for what seemed like hours. The management was worried that the stage might collapse. It was an incredible, uplifting evening, one that few people there will ever forget.

Years later, I heard from one of the organizers of the conference. "After Shlomo said that you were 'disgustingly Jewish,' I said to myself, 'You sure are!' Then I looked at myself, and said, 'And so am I!' It was the beginning of my return to my Jewish roots and tradition." She actually went on to become religious, and after years of following a more monastic, meditative path, she married and had children.

How did Shlomo know how to get into her heart? And how many countless others did he touch that evening?

55

SRI PAD:
A Reunion

After the conference in Bombay, I traveled to Vrindavan to see my old teacher. I hadn't been with him in ten years and I wasn't a sadhu anymore. I was an Orthodox rabbi with a family. I was planning to stay overnight and I was a little concerned about where I would sleep (inside or out?), and how I would sleep (on the ground or on a bed), and how and where I'd go to the toilet. Most important, how would Sri Pad receive me?

I took a taxi the couple of hours from the airport and arrived anxious and excited. Sri Pad didn't look that different, though he had aged. The fact was, I never knew how old he was. From stories I had heard about him when I was there before, he was a lot older than he appeared. Everyone certainly agreed that he was a very old and wise soul, regardless of the body he was in.

What had changed were his surroundings. Though he was still a sadhu, he had created an institution to preserve and translate ancient teachings. There were rooms for offices and meetings, and guest rooms, and even bathrooms.

The man was the same, and though his environs were drastically different than a decade before, I was touched, moved, and happy—deep in my soul—upon seeing him again. We had been in touch by letters sporadically over the years, but seeing him was something else. We spent a lot of time talking to each other. I tried to catch him up on all my activities in transpersonal psychology, on becoming a rabbi, and about starting my own organization, the Network of Conscious Judaism, to revive and teach the spiritual dimensions of Judaism.

From time to time, people came in to see him: dignitaries; common people, mainly Indians; some Westerners. Each time, we would pause. He would talk to them about whatever they had come to him for (advice or to receive his blessing), and he would always introduce me, in Hindi or in English. He was so proud to say that I had been a sadhu here many years ago and that now I was a rabbi. And he asked me to sing to him my songs from Judaism. I was thrilled at his openness, his interest, and his pleasure in my Hasidic songs. He loved the song of Rebbe Nachman's "Narrow Bridge" and asked me to sing it over and over:

All the world is just a narrow bridge, just a narrow
  bridge, just a narrow bridge.
All the world is just a narrow bridge, just a narrow bridge.
And above all, and above all, is not to fear, not to fear at all.
And above all, and above all, is not to fear at all.

I left feeling very validated about who I had become. Could he love me more as a rabbi than as a sadhu? I don't know, but having his blessing meant a great deal to me.

———

Several months later I got a letter from him. He had officially established his research project and included a few flyers about it. And there it was: *the Network of Krishna Consciousness*! He had liked the name of my organization so much that he had adapted it for his own. I didn't feel plagiarized. I felt honored that I was able to give something back to him after all that he had given to me.

I didn't know it then, but that would be my last meeting with my Blessed Sri Pad.

56

Reb Yisrael Odesser: The Spirit of Rebbe Nachman

While in Los Angeles in 1983 visiting my mother, I heard through the grapevine that there was a Hasidic rebbe in town from Israel who sounded interesting. His name was Reb Yisrael Odesser, and he was somehow connected to Breslov. I wouldn't call myself a "card-carrying" member of Breslov, but I felt very connected to Rebbe Nachman of Breslov from all I had received from both Reb Shlomo and Reb Gedaliah. I told my family that I was going out to meet some rebbe, and that I'd be back in an hour or so. They were fairly upset when I returned four hours later, but time had just evaporated while I was with him.

Reb Yisrael was very old. His gray hair was a tangle, his *peyot*, or side curls, were askew, and his broad, round-rimmed, black hat sat at an angle. His clothes were wrinkled. He wore his *tzitzit*, his garment with the fringes on the four corners, over his shirt, and an old long black coat over it. He sat hunched over, but his eyes were dancing, his face was illuminated with joy, and he was telling stories about his youth to the few followers and visitors sitting closely around him.

He came from an extremely poor family from Tiberias, a lovely town along the Sea of Galilee. His father was blind, and his mother baked and sold bread from flour that someone donated each week to support the family. He went to a religious school for poor children.

Despite his struggle just to survive physically, he had a much bigger struggle in his life. He knew there had to be a way to pray from the deepest depths of the heart, with a longing and an enthusiasm and a fire. But whenever he asked his rabbis and teachers about this, they told him it was nonsense, and he should just get on with simply saying the words of prayer, then return to his studies. He begged to learn more, but they just ridiculed him.

One day he found a Hebrew book whose cover pages had been torn off. It was lying in a garbage heap. That was no place for a holy book, so he picked it up and examined it curiously.

After looking at the first page, young Yisrael started trembling with excitement, with awe, with fear. The book was about how to really pray to God, how to *talk* to God. It taught about going out into the fields to talk to God, about praying with the trees. This book was the answer to his prayers. He devoured it from missing cover to missing cover. He read it over and over again. But why was the book torn? And why was it in the garbage? And who wrote it?

Reading the book one day in his yeshiva room, one of his roommates came in, grabbed the book from him, and said, "What's this you're reading?"

He looked closer, recognized the book, and said, "This is trash! Where did you get this? These are the forbidden teachings of Rebbe Nachman of Breslov! Don't you know better than to read this?" He took the book and ran out the door with it.

Yisrael was devastated. No sooner had he found the answer to his longing than it was cruelly snatched away from him. What could he do? At least now he knew who had written these inspired teachings. With the little that he had learned, he went out into the fields and poured out his soul to God—not speaking words from the prayer book, but speaking his own words, in his own language, and from the depths of his heart. "*Rebono Shel Olam*, Master of the World! I've waited so long to learn how to pray to You with love and awe, and finally You send me a book I can learn from. Then You take it away from me before I get a chance to learn it! Please send me another book, or send me a teacher who can help me. Please don't leave me like this."

Day after day, week after week, Yisrael prayed like this. No response.

Then one day, he was out walking and saw someone slumped over on a donkey, barely holding on. The man was very sick and weak, but he managed to whisper that he needed something to eat. Yisrael sensed that he was a very holy man, a *tzaddik*. Somehow he knew that God had sent him.

Yisrael took him to his mother. Although she hardly had enough to feed her own family, they took him in and cared for him, nursing him back to health. When he was a little stronger, they went for walks and got to know one another.

The old man was Reb Yisrael Karduner, from Sefat, where he had a print shop. Among other things, he printed the books of Rebbe Nachman. He spent most of his time in Meron, at the holy grave of Rabbi Shimon bar Yochai, praying as he had learned from the teachings of Rebbe Nachman. Now he had become very ill, but felt that he couldn't leave his holy place of prayer even for the sake of his health. So he kept putting off leaving, even temporarily, to come to Tiberias and soak in the healing hot springs. He had resisted and resisted for weeks until his condition was so precarious that he was forced to come down from the mountain.

He was the answer to Yisrael's prayers. Not only did he print the books of Rebbe Nachman, but his life and practice also had been deeply influenced by him. The two of them spent a great deal of time together, and Yisrael learned everything he could from him about the secrets of prayer and about the teachings of Rebbe Nachman.

Years later, in a moment of feeling far from God, Yisrael Odesser did not fast on an important fast day. After that he felt so bad about it that he didn't know what to do. He fasted and prayed, asking for help and guidance. Something told him to open one of his books and look for an answer in it.

He pulled out a book by Rebbe Nachman and opened it randomly. He read what was written, but couldn't see that it answered his questions. But there was a piece of folded paper in the book. Yisrael moved it out of the way, and read what was written on the facing page. Again, he found no answer. He read it a few more times. Nothing. Finally, he picked up the paper and looked at it. It was a letter in Rebbe Nachman's handwriting—a message from beyond time and space. Mentioning that he hadn't fasted on that particular day, Rebbe Nachman was telling him not to give up. It was signed in a way that no one had ever seen before: Na Nach Nachma Nachman M' (from) Uman.

This revelation for Reb Yisrael became the foundation of the rest of his life and of his teachings. Today, a whole movement within Breslov Hasidism is based on this. For them, "Na Nach Nachma Nachman M'Uman" is a powerful mantra.

When Reb Yisrael finished telling this story to me, he began telling stories of Rebbe Nachman. Now, I had heard these stories from Reb Shlomo and Reb Zalman and Reb Gedaliah. They are powerful, and I learned tremendously from them. But no one told them like Reb Yisrael. It was as if he were telling it for the first time, blowing his mind on every word, on every image. He was also blowing my mind with every word and every image.

For instance, when telling part of Rebbe Nachman's story of the Seven Beggars, where one beggar was telling of his ability to heal the princess who had been shot with arrows, Reb Yisrael said, "The beggar said, 'And *I* could heal the princess.' And when Rebbe Nachman said that, he pointed to himself, and he said, 'And *I* could heal the princess.'" And while Reb Yisrael spoke, I could feel the healing coming through. Why did he pick that one short part of Rebbe Nachman's longest story? Did he know that my wife Ety had cancer and was struggling to be healed?

As he told story after story, or just certain parts of the stories that he knew needed to be told, I lost all sense of time.

I met with him a number of times after that, but that first meeting was the most powerful. He had an energy, a love, a joy that was totally beyond his old and frail physical body.

Na Nach Nachma Nachman M'Uman. Na Nach Nachma Nachman M'Uman!

57

THE AMSHINOVER REBBE: Beyond Time

In the summer of 1985, I was leading a very small tour of Israel. I wanted people not only to see where everyone from our illustrious past was dead and buried, but also to see where people and places were alive *today*. I wanted them to meet a Judaism that was dynamic, alive, and well. In a world where everyone was running to teachers and gurus from various spiritual and mystical and meditative traditions *except* Judaism, I wanted them to meet Hasidic and kabbalistic rebbes and masters. I wanted them to meet artists and musicians who were delving deeply into their creativity through their Judaism. I wanted them to know that these people exist and feel their presence and their light and their love.

The tour was called "Timeless Tours." We planned to meet mainly with teachers and artists whom I knew, including Rav Sheinberger, Rav Adin Steinsaltz, and Reb Gedaliah's son, Reb Elazar Kenig.

I had heard of the Amshinover Rebbe from Shlomo and other friends. Though I didn't know him, he sounded like another good deep well for my students to drink from. I heard that he sort of lived beyond time. He might do his morning prayers late in the afternoon, and he might still be observing Shabbat long past Saturday night. In fact, at Shlomo's funeral, which was on a Monday, some of the Amshinover's Hasidim apologized for the Rebbe's absence because he was still in Shabbat.

But that's getting beyond the time of this story.

When I got to Israel, I called the phone number I had for the Rebbe and asked to speak to him. "Speaking," he said. This was quite surprising, as most rebbes have someone manage their affairs or screen their phone calls.

"My name is David Zeller," I said. "I'm a Hasid of Shlomo Carlebach. I'm leading a small tour of Americans to show them the living tradition of Judaism and that Jewish mysticism and spirituality are alive and well in Israel. We are visiting different holy places, but most important, we are meeting with as many inspiring rabbis and teachers as we can. I would like to bring the group to meet with you."

"That sounds like a wonderful idea for a tour of Israel," he said, "but why do you want to meet with me?"

"Because I'm trying to expose my group to Jewish teachers and rebbes who live and teach from that depth of Jewish spirituality and mysticism. I understand that you are very busy and may not have the time for this. Or maybe you may not believe in meeting with not-so-religious people like this. But I think it's very important for them."

"Yes, I understand, and I have lots of time," he said. "But why do you want to see *me*?"

I remember that conversation so well. I took the phone away from my ear and looked at it in astonishment, bewilderment, and consternation, thinking to myself, "Who *is* this man? Is he for real?" Or was he so humble that he didn't realize that he was one of those rebbes that I was talking about?

I continued my conversation. "We want to see you because *you* are one of those spiritual teachers we are seeking to meet with."

"Oh," he said, surprised at what I'd said. "Well, if you want to meet with me, of course I have the time."

And he met with us, spoke with the whole group, and then took time out for a private meeting with each person in the group.

Over the years, I have seen the Rebbe a number of times, by myself and with others whom I thought he could help. I have taken many classes in psychology and in developing listening skills and compassion. But I never learned as much as I have with the Amshinover Rebbe. He sits quite close and listens so intently, with his entire being. He listens to your heart and your soul. He hears how the heart is really feeling, and he tunes in to what your soul is saying and praying. He goes far beyond the thoughts in your mind and the words of your speech. And he keeps on listening as long as you keep speaking. I can't remember him ever interrupting someone to give an answer, or to say, "Okay, I hear what the problem is, now listen to me.... " I never heard him say, "You're repeating yourself.... "

He keeps on listening even after you stop talking. He sits in silence, your silence, his silence, and he still listens, still tuned in: his heart and soul to your heart and soul.

Once I brought someone to talk to the Rebbe who talked at great length, without any interruption. It seemed she misunderstood the Rebbe's silence for needing to hear more, or maybe she was just suffering from the discomfort that many people have with silence. The Rebbe would not interrupt this outpouring of words. Rather, he kept listening conscientiously and attentively. It didn't matter how many other people might be sitting outside in the "waiting room," or that it was already 3 a.m. He was going to hear you all the way through, and hear all the way through you.

After I had seen the Rebbe a few times myself, I learned to prepare. I tried to listen to myself first. Was the question I had or the problem I was dealing with the real question or the real problem? Could I listen more deeply to myself, to my heart and my soul? What was the real issue and concern of my soul? What is my soul's real story? Where am I in the unfolding of my soul's story and purpose?

I usually met with him in the middle of the night, as he teaches all day in schools and yeshivas, then spends time with his family. You'd think this would fatigue him. But I've learned that fatigue from being up late is nothing compared to the fatigue of being "off" and far from your soul's purpose. Nothing tires the soul more than being off our path and far from our story and our purpose. He was so close to the essence of his being that he was truly an awakened master.

58

ELANA:
Coming to Israel to Stay

I had applied for a rabbinical position in the Boston area, because Ety, who now called herself Elana, wanted to be closer to her family, who lived on the East Coast. She had chosen the name Elana because it was closer to Elaine than the Yiddish Ety, but more so because it meant "tree," and she had developed a special relationship to trees during her healing. Now that her cancer was in remission, she was ready for a change in name and location. I was about to leave for Israel to lead a three-week summer "mystical tour." At the last minute, her brother generously bought tickets for her and our children, saying that she should have the joy of visiting Israel after her heroic battle for her life.

While I was with the tour, I got the call from Boston that I had been approved for the job by the synagogue's board. I told them to call back tomorrow after I discussed it with my wife. I phoned her immediately. "I got the job as rabbi," I said hesitantly, "but, are we going back?"

"No," she said, very naturally, "we're not going back."

And that was that. We had come with just a few small suitcases for all of us. We'd planned to be there for only one month. Very quickly, we chose where to live, and gathered more of the necessities we would need to stay for at least a year. After focusing my life around her healing for the past two years, she offered me this year in Israel so I could sit and learn in yeshiva, a luxury I had never had.

We settled in Efrat. Why Efrat? Because, she said, "We are not living where we feel like living. We will live close to where *you* will be learning. I don't want you spending an hour or more each day commuting. Find the best place for your learning, and everything will fall into place." When we found the yeshiva of Rabbi Brovender and Rabbi Riskin, a place open to Shlomo and his Hasidim—and when they accepted me to come and learn there—we knew we had found the right place. And everyone there loved Elana and her joy and her art. And she loved the people of Israel and being in the Judean hills.

Then the cancer came back with a vengeance—to her liver. Because of her joyous nature and radiant personality, the doctors dismissed her symptoms. "You don't *look* sick!" they said. Precious time was lost until they saw through her aura and found the cancer. And then they refused to tell her the real diagnosis and prognosis, feeling ethically that they couldn't tell her how serious and fatal it was. We both fought with them to know the truth. "If I don't know how serious it is, I can't know how hard I have to fight it," she said. At last they gave in and told her it was just a matter of months. And did *she* fight it. And even with that hanging over her, she would not be rushed or pushed into things. She still admonished me, "Use your Shabbos voice. Walk your Shabbos walk." Where others might start to race through whatever time they had to try to do as much as they could fit in, she would say, "I don't have time to hurry."

She danced and sang and painted and took chemotherapy and brewed her Chinese herbal teas. She embraced me and our children and God—with all her heart, with all her soul, and with all her strength. And for every measure that God measured out to her, she gave thanks, very, very much. But the cancer was unrelenting.

The community of Efrat was incredibly supportive. Meals were prepared and brought to the house every day, for lunch and dinner, for more than half a year. Teenagers came to help take care of the children, clean the house, and more. One time they cleaned out our refrigerator and told us how they found something that looked like a long rat tail, and threw it out. It was our precious burdock root, for our macrobiotic healing diet. But their love and efforts to help were far more healing. People would just knock on the door and hand us envelopes with money, saying that there must be so many unexpected and hidden costs to pay for. People actually thanked us for letting them into our lives and letting them help. I learned that the mitzvah of *bikur cholim*, visiting the sick, has two sides: the one who wants to visit, and the sick person who needs to let him in.

Shlomo came to Efrat for a Shabbat especially for her, and did a *tish*, "a rebbes's table," on Friday night. It started the tradition of his coming to Efrat for a Shabbat once a year, which led, years later, to starting the first weekly Carlebach minyan outside his shul in Manhattan and on the moshav.

We went to see a psychologist, a specialist in death and dying. When he looked at her with his sad and sympathetic eyes, she stood up and marched out of the room, like the rebbe who was carried into the *beit midrash*, the study hall, literally on his death bed. They set his bed on the tabletops, and his students were standing around him crying. He was no longer able to speak, so he wrote a note saying, "All my life I've worked so hard to be happy. Please! Don't spoil my last moments! Dance!" And they danced and they sang and they danced some more. And when they looked up, he had passed away peacefully and happily.

I remember the children getting upset with their mother because as she became more sick, she needed me more, and I couldn't be with them as much as I had been. We both tried to explain to them that it was only because she had become sick in the first place that I was home with them at all. "Before Ima got sick, Abba was always out on lecture tours or teaching away from home. He gave it up only when I got sick, so that he could take care of you. At first I was still strong enough to take care of myself. But now, I'm so sorry, I need him, too."

At last, she sent me to buy "good-bye for a lifetime" gifts for the children: a *siddur* (prayer book), for each one, imprinted with their names, and Shabbat candlesticks for Manya and Esther and a Kiddush cup for Mordechai. But she didn't want to give them—yet. She was still holding out for that last great chapter of healing and of victory.

She had her first art exhibit in the Gush Eztion Community Center. The town council of Efrat bought her sketch of Natan Sharansky embracing his wife as he got off the plane in Israel after his release from Russia. They wanted to present it to Sharansky when he visited Efrat in a few weeks. So Elana lived to see her fulfillment as an artist: having an exhibit and selling her work.

Then the day came. She said it was time to give the children their presents. She called them in, one at a time, starting with the oldest. To each, she said, "You know I've been very sick, and God willing, I'm going to get better. But a lot of people die from this, and I might die, too. I want you to know that just because I have this doesn't mean that you will. And though sometimes we parents say stupid things like, 'You make me sick when you act like that....' believe me, *you* didn't make me sick. No one has the power to make another person sick." Then she looked her or him lovingly in the eyes and said, "God willing I'm going to get better. But is there anything you want to ask me or tell me?"

Manya, who was eight, was old enough to know these things can happen and shouldn't happen. She was also old enough to need to be in denial. She said, "I don't have anything to ask because I know you're going to get better." She needed to protect her very vulnerable and frightened self. But in school, she had drawn a picture of a circus trapeze artist, hanging from her trapeze by one toe....

Mordechai, who was five, was young enough to accept what was happening as natural, and to express what was socially forbidden. He asked straightforwardly, "After you die, will Abba get married again?" It was as if he were tuned in to *his* and the family's continuity. We both took a deep breath and she answered, "Of course, if I die, Abba will marry again so you will have a good mother who will take care of you."

And then Esther, who was three, so young as to be beyond this world, answered her mother's statement by asking, "Did you tell God what you want to be?"

"Of course," Elana answered, "I told God I want to be healthy."

"No," Esther corrected her, "Did you tell God what you want to be *after* you die?!" We looked at each other astonished. She was so young that she could be tuned in to her *mother's* continuity.

Elana died a few days later. Family came from America, and our Carlebach and Efrat friends streamed in. Shlomo led the *levaya*, the funeral service. He had married us, and now he was burying her. I don't remember what he said. I'm not sure exactly where I was other than mourning my loss and worrying about the children and trying to be with them and protect them as much as possible. I just remember that Shlomo had his arm around me the whole time he spoke.

That week, Sharansky was given the picture. Of course, he asked who the artist was. When they told him she had just died, he said, "Then her family must be sitting shiva. Please take me to them." And he came to pay his respects.

Elana was like a salmon who had swum upstream, against the flow, to lay her eggs and die. She brought her children to their true home and Source of All Life, before letting go of her own life.

59

RAV MORDECHAI SHEINBERGER: A Real Kabbalist and a Real Human Being

Earlier, whenever I made the trip from the United States to Israel, I was always searching for basic classic texts of Kabbalah and Hasidism for my Network bookstore. On one such trip, in 1983, I was introduced to Rav Mordechai Sheinberger. He lived in the Old City of Jerusalem, dressed in the long black coat and round-brimmed black hat of the ultra-Orthodox, was very kind and friendly, and had sparkling blue eyes. He had the Hebrew texts I was looking for: *Etz Chaiim*, ("The Tree of Life") and the multivolumed *Sha'arim* ("The Gateways") containing the teachings of the *Ari z"l*, Rabbi Yitzhak Lurie, of Sefat. In addition, he had Rav Ashlag's *HaSulam* ("The Ladder"), the multivolume explanation of the Zohar, and a separate set of volumes on the Ten Sefirot. He also had many books I had never heard of.

Not until years later did I discover he wasn't really a book dealer, but a teacher—and a kabbalist. After Reb Gedaliah passed away, I began to really appreciate Rav Sheinberger. When I led my tour group to Israel in 1985, he was one of the teachers I brought them to. And later, when I brought Ram Dass and other teachers to Israel, I always made sure that they had time to get to know him.

For a number of years after I moved to Israel, I was with him for Rosh HaShanah and Yom Kippur, where he took a classroom space in the Old City of Jerusalem for his minyan to pray in. His prayers were full of beautiful melodies and were very uplifting. He was a "real" rebbe, with quite a sweet community that prays with him at the Holy Western Wall every Shabbat and gathers at his home for a Kiddush every Shabbat morning. Several years ago, a group of his followers started a cooperative community near Sefat—*Ohr HaGanuz*, "the Hidden Light." Their lives are based on the most important and basic of all kabbalistic teachings and practices: Love your Neighbor/Friend/Beloved as your Self.

But when did I discover that Rav Sheinberber was a *tzaddik*—a holy person? It was in the 1990s, at the wedding of the daughter of friends of mine. It was during the dancing around the *chatan* and *callah,* the groom and the bride. The rebbe took off his glasses and his hat, handed them to one of his students, and began to dance and to turn summersaults with freedom and joy. There was no inhibition, no self-consciousness, no holding on to his airs as rebbe and serious kabbalist. He was able to change roles like the High Priest changing clothes going in and out of the Holy of Holies. And then, he got on the stage with the band, took a microphone, and sang along with them.

His unassuming freedom won me over more than anything I had ever learned from him. He didn't have to get high to reach the place where he could free himself of the constraints of his dignity, to clown around, or to let loose. He was a rebbe in everything he did, whether teaching, leading prayers, or turning summersaults. He didn't stop being one in order to be the other.

Many people need to drink something or take something to "liberate" themselves from their dominant identity. But if you still see your various roles as separate, different, or limiting, it's a sign that you're not really, fully, truly who you can be.

I remember talking to a friend and teacher about how much I love teaching and singing, and how present and in the flow I feel when doing it. And I spoke about the wear and tear of getting from one teaching or concert to the next and how exhausting that part of the work can be.

He said, "You should feel as present and in the flow when you are traveling as you are when you are singing. If not, you are still living in duality, in multiple identities, and you are not yet whole unto yourself. God is with you wherever you are and whatever you are doing. Now it's time for *you* to be with God wherever you are and whatever you are doing."

It is so important to stop and reflect from time to time along the way. As I get more "spiritual," am I taking myself too seriously? Was meditation creating separations and distinctions in parts of my being or was it the means through which the different parts of my Self could become united? For me, Rav Sheinberger is a significant lighthouse and guidepost and rebbe along the way.

60

HANNAH-SARA:
Life After Death

Elana had said that if she died, I would get married again, and that the children would have a good and caring mother. But I was still dealing with my loss and wondering whether I could find someone else I could love, and who could love and understand me. Or should I just find someone who would be the best mother or caretaker for my children? Various people were proposing possible matches for me and I was meeting lots of women in my professional capacity as teacher, rabbi, and singer. Almost two years had gone by, and I had pursued a couple of serious prospects for several months, but one called it off, and another time I called it off. It just wasn't the right fit.

Then I met *her*, and she seemed to be who I had been looking for. She seemed so right. But it was at a workshop, and I was on my professional best behavior. I let the opportunity pass. Two months later, I got a phone call from a rabbi friend who said, "David, I just met your soul mate! When can you meet her?"

"One of my kids has chicken pox, and I've got family here from the States," I said. "It's not a good time."

"I don't care what's going on, you make the time to meet her now, while she's still in Israel."

It was *her*, again. We met, a little shy, a little scared, and a lot of barely contained excitement. There was something mysterious or hidden just below the surface about her. She was reflective and sensitive and contemplative. She was also hesitant and cautious after ending her own marriage more than ten years ago. And I was hesitant and cautious after suffering the loss of a wonderful marriage, just two years earlier.

We took time to hear each other's story. The third time we met, I tried to take her for a picnic, but I got lost and couldn't find where I was looking for. We wound up back in Jerusalem, in the parking lot of a hotel. We had our picnic there, sitting on a rock, under a tree. And who should come by? Shlomo Carlebach! He took a good look at the two of us. "Ah," he said, "now you've found the princess." And in the blink of an eye, he was gone.

It was scary for each of us to think we could really love again. But we were quite a match. Her name was Wendy Shapiro. She had been a pre-med student at Reed College in Portland, Oregon. But her interest in art led her to a class in Zen calligraphy taught by a visiting Zen master, Suzuki Roshi. That led to regular Zen meditation, and the hours of intense sitting led to her awareness of chronic back pain, which led her to study yoga. Eventually, she become a yoga teacher under the training of Swami Satchitananda, who also brought her to a more devotional/heart approach to spirituality then Zen had. Swami Satchitananda had the same teacher as Swami Radha and Swami Vishnu Devananda. Swami Satchitananda also sponsored various interfaith gatherings. That's how Wendy came to know Rabbi Carlebach. Slowly, she moved back into Judaism. In fact, the first time I saw her was at a workshop I was teaching together with Shlomo and other New York rabbis.

If all those common overlaps weren't enough, her father had been the family pediatrician for the early American folk legend Woody Guthrie. And my own pre-med major had led me to Berkeley, and my love for Woody and folk music had led me to the Berkeley Folk Festival, which had led me to Shlomo.

But Wendy, who changed her name to Hannah-Sara when we got married, had also suffered many losses. At the age of three, she lost a finger on a department store escalator. At eighteen, she lost her father to cancer. That set her adrift from her earlier direction in life, and to a certain degree, from her family. But it was her first marriage—which ended badly, followed by her ex-husband kidnapping her daughter—that was her greatest loss.

She spent nearly a year in a Zen retreat center where Baker Roshi helped her pick up the pieces of her life and gain the strength, the determination, and the chutzpah to go and get her daughter back. With her mother's help, she hired a private detective and tracked them to India, where the father was holding the daughter captive. Risking her life and every penny she had, they set up a "sting" operation and got her four-year-old back.

When she first returned to the United States, Baker Roshi sent her to one of his teachers, who often came to his Zen center to give workshops in sensory awareness—Charlotte Selver! Charlotte lived on a secluded island in Maine, and Charlotte and her island provided Wendy with a much-needed renewal of spirit. It was a perfect environment for mother and daughter to re-bond after a long and traumatic separation.

Needless to say, her daughter's father began an aggressive search for her. Wendy changed her name and social security number and they lived in hiding. Several times he tracked them down. With just hours of warning, she managed to pack up and drive into the night to a new location. Eventually he died, and they were free, thank God, to live their lives fully.

Walking barefoot in the dark, like I did, is one way to face the unknown and find God's loving shelter. Fleeing into the night to an unknown destination for fear of your life, like Hannah-Sara did, is something totally different. The loss of safety, security, trust, and shelter—and its accompanying fear—leave deep imprints that are all too easily *re-lived* and not so easily *relieved*.

All this was the source of that more quiet, melancholy, deeply sensitive, still-ready-to-run side that I had sensed in this woman I had fallen in love with.

I courted her with my own homemade chocolate chip cookies. Later, she enticed me with her international culinary skills with Indian, Chinese, and Mexican food. It was a re-match made in heaven: common interests and experiences in Eastern practices and meditation; American folk music; and most important, our love of spirituality, Judaism, and Shlomo. Did I say most important? No, most important to both of us was our children. She had her daughter, Meera, and I had my three younger children, Manya, Mordechai, and Esther. We were really looking to make a new home for all of us.

She went back to the United States and her job as an art teacher at a Jewish day school, and I continued teaching psychology, mysticism, and meditation at various centers in Israel. We courted each other long distance, mainly through letters and rare phone calls. We decided that she should come back with her daughter Meera so all of us could decide about being together. They came for Hanukkah in 1988, and we all got along great. We went to my closest friends, David and Shoshana Cooper, for Shabbat. We were sitting in the dark—Mordechai on my lap and Esther on Meera's lap—talking about how we could merge our lives here in Israel. My daughter, Manya, who had been the most reluctant, came in, sat in *Wendy's* lap (!) and joined in the conversation. I asked her, "Do you understood what we're talking about?" "Yes," she answered matter-of-factly, "you're talking about getting married and living together here in Israel." Shoshana stuck her head in the room for a moment, saw what was happening, glowed, and disappeared, knowing this was a time for us to feel what it was like really being together.

Rabbi Shlomo and Rabbi Meir Fund married us in June 1989, in the Rose Garden of the Brooklyn Botanical Gardens. We held it there so many of our American family could attend. We had our honeymoon on a yacht crewed by the Coopers, sailing through the Caribbean islands. Then we came home, and our new family settled in Efrat.

It was a new beginning for everyone. "Wendy" again changed her name, but this time not because she was in hiding but to finally come home and blossom in the sun. She was now Hannah-Sara Zeller. She had to learn a new language and adjust to a family of four children, three of them still quite young. Meera had to adjust to an Israeli high school where *everything* was taught in Hebrew. Her biggest adjustment was sharing her mother with three younger siblings. But she gained two sisters and a brother in the deal, and it seemed to be a good trade-off.

Within the first year, Hannah-Sara had taken a half a year of Jewish studies, followed by a Hebrew language intensive *ulpan*. Then she spent some unusual time with a gas mask over her head with the rest of the family in our "sealed room," during the Iraqi missile attacks. Talk about family bonding. She really devoted herself to the children, knowing they hadn't had a mother for a significant part of their childhood. The kids literally ate it up, as the cooking improved considerably, along with the love and attention.

Hannah-Sara had to push me out of the kitchen (the kids helped her do that) and out of the house (a more difficult task for the kids) to go back to my teaching and lecture tours. With her support at home, I could give myself more to developing my work in Israel and my lecture and concert tours abroad. I created several *beit midrash* programs of learning, each drawing from a variety of Jewish mystical texts, each with a different focus: one in psychology, one in Hasidism, and one in meditation. It stretched my learning and teaching to much higher levels.

Despite the fears of the Gulf War and the Intifada, she gave birth to and raised our son Sha'arya, in addition to the children we already had. She integrated her years of yoga with her Torah study, becoming the "Mother" of a whole new approach to teaching yoga called "Torah-Yoga." She has taught this in many religious women's programs and at yoga retreats. She started teaching creative art and movement to the senior citizens in our area, and more and more she was asked to do art

for *ketubot* (wedding contracts) for my CD covers, for children's books, and for a wide range of projects. As she integrated Torah into yoga, so she integrated Torah, Judaism, and
Israel into her art. Her unique style captured the beauty of the
Judean hills, their shrubs, rocks, and stone dwellings, while
weaving in images of Jerusalem and the Holy Temple.

Hannah-Sara made the Holy Days come alive like never
before. She loved applying her artistic talents to designing the
most beautiful *sukkah*. From the original scenes she painted
on each of the sheet walls, to delightful overhead hangings and
lights, to the pillows and cushions, she created a magical and
majestic space that we all slept and ate in. For Purim she could
turn the kids' wildest ideas into the most wonderful costumes.
She has been a constant resource and inspiration in the family
and in the community for creative solutions to art projects, set
designs, costumes, and recipes. Together with our friends in
Efrat, we helped start the Carlebach "Happy Minyan." Like
Betsy Ross and the American flag, Hannah-Sara sewed the
curtain for the synagogue, and helped with so many other
aspects of the shul's needs in the early years.

As the children grew up, went to live-in high schools,
yeshivas, colleges, and programs, and more or less moved out,
they came home with more and more friends, offering it as a
place to crash on their way from here to there. There has rarely
been a dull or empty moment, and Hannah-Sara always looks
forward to the stories and songs these newcomers add to our
table, along with her delicious meals.

Her other great gift is music. Sometimes, though not nearly
enough, we pull out our instruments—me and my guitar and
her and her mandolin—and we start with Shlomo songs, and
eventually go back to our roots in folk music, and back again
to Shlomo. These are the most healing moments for all of us.
Holy Days and Shabbat are special, but they require a lot of
preparation. Music can be so much more spontaneous.

Hannah-Sara also participates in amazing women's activities, such as the monthly New Moon gathering at the
Carlebach Moshav, with prayer, singing, yoga, dance, learning,

eating, and every kind of new creative approach to Judaism and life.

We have shared many special moments together in our home, in our Efrat community, and in our extended Carlebach community—singing and dancing at bar and bat mitzvahs and at weddings, and crying together at funerals and memorials. In and out of Intifadas, living with fear about her own safety or the safety of her children and grandchildren, Hannah-Sara continues to rise to the occasion.

61

RAM DASS IN ISRAEL: The Form and the Formless

Not long after seeing Ram Dass at that memorial lecture in Los Angeles, he informed me that he had a workshop in Europe and would use that as an opportunity to come to Israel. I made the arrangements for several phases of his visit. I wanted him to see much of Israel, its beauty, its history, and its people—religious and nonreligious. I wanted him to meet teachers and rebbes. I wanted him to experience Shabbat in the Old City of Jerusalem and in Meah Sha'arim. And I wanted him to give some of his own teachings over a few evenings that would be open to the general public. He was open to whatever and whoever and wherever.

We met with Rabbi Mordechai Sheinberger in the Old City, who received him graciously and respectfully. They spoke of meditation as a way to know God, and of perceptions, insights, and understandings that each had arrived at in his own way. It wasn't a contest or a debate. It was an open, respectful dialogue.

Often, while visiting yeshivas, meeting in people's homes, and walking on the street, we ran into people who acknowledged that Ram Dass had been a significant turning point in their lives and their spiritual journey. Some wished they could convince him to join them in the Judaism that their quest had led them to; some were just grateful for his wisdom that had helped point the way back home for them.

We took several days to travel to northern Israel. We went to Sefat and took a ritual bath in the ice-cold natural *mikvah* of Rabbi Yitzhak Luria, the great kabbalist of the sixteenth century. Then we met with Rabbi Elazar Kenig, the son of Reb Gedaliah, who was now the spiritual head of the Sefat Breslov community that his father had begun. Again, the meeting was gentle and respectful. No one was berating Ram Dass for the path he had chosen. Everyone just compared and honored discoveries and differences.

Meeting with other Jews was as important as meeting with these rebbes. As we traveled the land, we were always talking: it was sometimes light, sometimes heavy; sometimes teasing, sometimes serious. We kept making stops along the way for archeological digs and ancient Jewish communities and synagogues that went back thousands of years. Ram Dass would question this fixation with the past, with history, with the dead. It seemed so contrary to the Buddhist perspective of becoming free from samsara, from the debts of one's past, and of one's past lives. It was part of the ongoing dialogue between Jewish tradition of thousands of years and the spirituality of the here and now, between the Buddhist nothing and the Jewish everything. There were so many words, props, and paraphernalia compared to the silence and simplicity of pure meditation. In his words, it was the dance between the "form" and the "formless."

Then we visited Stephen Folder, a Jew originally from England, with a PhD in biochemistry. Stephen was an expert in herbology and alternative medicine, and a leading teacher in Israel of the Buddhist practice of Vipassana, or mindfulness meditation.

Their discussion included a wide range of teachers in India and elsewhere with whom they had both studied over the years. It was a lively, relaxed, and comfortable exchange—two "dharma brothers" on the same path, speaking the same language. Ram Dass felt truly at home.

Then they shifted their focus to the various practices they each had done or were doing, as they both talked of the amount of time spent in meditation. At one point, Stephen talked about a particular retreat, where after intense meditation, he felt the natural flow going into Jewish prayer. He talked about how from the depth of the meditation of the "formless" came the appreciation and awe of creation, of all of existence, where he found prayer to be the perfect "form" for expressing that appreciation. And he talked about Shabbat (the Sabbath), and *shavat* (cessation), which he has observed for years, as Judaism's practice of formlessness.

As we went from discussing Buddhist practice to Jewish practice, from the formless to the form, the whole atmosphere and consciousness in the room was transformed and heightened. For me, the room seemed to change color and was saturated with a presence as Ram Dass said, "You pray? You practice Shabbat?" As if to say, "You found form in the formless? You found the formless in the Jewish form?"

It was a magical, eternal moment.

Later in the small community of Yodfat we met a young man who was the archetype of the rooted-in-the-earth Israeli. He had mussed, slightly long hair and just wore an undershirt and casual pants. He talked about his love of the land and riding bareback on his horse across the fields. I could imagine the sun rising as he galloped across its golden-red orb, his hair streaming in the wind. Then, with the same breath, he described how he goes once a week to Sefat, immerses himself in the Ari's holy *mikvah*, and prays in the Abuhav Synagogue!

Again the stereotypes burst as we found yet another person blending his nonreligious lifestyle with Jewish practice.

After our travels up north, we returned to Jerusalem, where I had arranged a small apartment for Ram Dass in the Old City. This gave him his own space and time to wander around alone if he wanted to. Since the Old City's many narrow winding walkways reminded me so much of Vrindavan, I thought he might also like that ancient, timeless atmosphere.

On Shabbat, we went to the Kotel, the Holy Wall, for kabbalat Shabbat, evening prayers. Then we had our meal at a private home, filled with people eager to reconnect with him and share their Jewish insights with him. Shabbat lunch was at another home, and then we took our Shabbat rest before heading to Meah Sha'arim, where we went to two different Hasidic communities. At Breslov, he got a taste of traditional Hasidim, but with quite a number of Baalei Tshuvas, those who had recently returned to a life of Torah. The learning, the singing, and the feeling was very high, and a few men came up to him and said, "Ram Dass? Is that you? I heard you back in the '70s, when I was just beginning my spiritual search."

At the Hasidic community of Slonim, in a large hall, we entered into a totally otherworldly dimension. Their attire— long black silk coats and round-rimmed black hats—made them look somewhat alike and similar to many other Hasidic groups. But the *niggunim,* their melodies, were totally different. In progressions of half-tones, in a scale from outer space, hundreds of Hasidim sang for hours in what must be a mind-altering, dronelike, meditative chant.

When we left the yeshiva, Ram Dass asked whether they experienced a carryover from this state of consciousness into the everyday. I told him that would vary from individual to individual, but that constantly working on one's *midot,* one's character traits and consciousness, was very strongly emphasized in the teachings of their lineage. The chanting was just a part of the whole picture of their spiritual practice.

At the end of his *tour de force* of Israel, Ram Dass gave an evening talk at my learning center, Yakar. The room was packed with a rainbow of Jews, from ultra-Orthodox in black hats and coats, to every color of *kipa* and headscarf, to no head covering.

What a rich tapestry of humanity he had inspired over the years and drew that night! From our earliest connection in Vrindavan to being his host in Israel, it was a true joy to show Ram Dass some of our "national treasures" of time (Shabbat), space (the Land of Israel), and being (the range of unusual people he met). My only hope was that he might now have more stories of Jewish time, space, and being to include in his wealth of stories from his own unfolding spiritual journey.

Only a few years later, his guru, as he put it, gave him a "Zen-wake-up-tap" in the form of a stroke, giving him a whole new pathway to negotiate.

62

Tending Our Garden of Peace

By far the most difficult and challenging art project in my wife Hannah-Sara's life was to feel secure and permanent enough—rooted—to plant a garden in our yard. Much of a home's interior you can pack up and take with you if you need. Not a garden. But after years in the house, Hannah-Sara finally sunk down those roots—literally—and created a wondrous garden, working together with our Arab friend, Ratib, from the village nearby. And there she was, going against the norm, risking her life as she went into open fields with "an Arab" to look for big, unusual rocks for the garden. They'd find something and somehow manage to get it into the car and back to the house. Or she would drive into his village for other cut stones for stepping-stones and benches. Over the years, it has developed into a glorious garden.

It really started years ago. Hannah-Sara's mother had been a teacher and guide at the Brooklyn Botanical Gardens for forty years, and a peace activist for even longer. She had planted many seeds in Hannah-Sara's soul, including a love of the earth and of all humanity. So, when Ratib came looking for odd jobs—building or renovating houses, or gardening—we really wanted to give him work. Sometimes he was just going door to door, selling delicious grapes from his family's vineyard. He offered to plant some grapes in our barren yard, and we agreed. Around then we added an apple, fig, and pomegranate tree. We always offered him coffee and something to eat; we got to know one another, a little. There wasn't always work and we couldn't always help him. Sometimes we had used household items and sometimes clothes his children could wear. We would make a deal: He would do a job that he estimated should require eight hours, and we agreed on a price after some bargaining. After all that, he would get the job done in two hours and still want all the money, and we'd argue some more. I'd get mad. He'd get mad. We'd both feel used and upset. I would think to myself, "Welcome to the Middle East, where peace can only be bargained for."

Then came the Intifada and greatly heightened security. After an aborted suicide bombing in our supermarket, Arabs weren't allowed into Efrat for quite some time. Ratib would call and ask how we were and whether we could buy a phone card for his mobile phone so he could stay in touch with his family and look for work opportunities. Or he'd call to say he had fresh vegetables from his garden he wanted to give us: tomatoes, cucumbers, cauliflower, squash, string beans, and some vegetables we'd never seen before. I'd drive out of Efrat and meet him on the road by his village. He'd get in the car and give me a hug and we'd kiss each other on both cheeks, and he'd give me a bag filled with the vegetables. He never asked for anything in return, and I would always give some money, far beyond its worth in the market. I had to laugh. All those years bargaining over the value of the work, and now just giving to each other whatever we could to help the other out.

When security eased up a bit, he could come and work, but there had to be an armed person watching him. It was painful for us, knowing the importance of the security, and yet feeling Ratib's suffering: not being trusted and not being able to provide for his family beyond what he could grow.

So when Hannah-Sara, with her mother's enthusiastic encouragement, started to really develop the garden before our youngest son Sha'arya's bar mitzvah, Ratib jumped at the opportunity to help. "I don't care what you pay me or when you pay me," he said. "You're like a brother to me. I just want to help." First he built a stone storage shed out in the far corner of our small backyard. He quoted fair prices and time schedules and met them. Hannah-Sara wanted an arbor for the grapes he had planted fifteen years earlier. He made all the arrangements and supervised the work. He noticed unfinished work from renovations to our house from five years earlier and fixed it. Whatever plants, mosses, and flowers she bought, he helped plant them. He was identified with the garden and its growth and development and with us. He would quote verses from the Koran or from poetry in Arabic and translate into Hebrew. He loved God and he loved the earth and all growing things.

He took such pride in the garden and brought other people to see it (also in the hopes they might hire him to do their garden). I paid him whatever I could and whenever I could. He knew we were having a bar mitzvah and a wedding at a time when I wasn't bringing in much income because I was sitting at home working on this book! But I knew that my low income and his low income were worlds apart.

In the middle of all this, Ratib's newest grandson was born with medical problems. Soon after that, his father had a stroke and needed considerable treatment and rehabilitation. Ratib had been saving a little money for the long bus ride to Mecca for his hajj, the Muslim pilgrimage to their holy city. He'd even asked me to buy him a nice, inexpensive suit from America. Now all his meager savings went to his grandson and his father, but it hardly scratched the surface.

When he came to our door looking for work and telling me about his grandfather who was going blind, or asking me about how my work was going, or how my children and grandchildren were, if I sighed in resignation because of the political situation or his situation, he would catch me and say, "It's forbidden to sigh in sadness! Everything is from God, and everything is in God's hands. You have to say 'Praise be to God.'" I have done a fair amount of Arab-Israeli and Muslim-Jewish dialogues, locally and internationally. But this is the real thing. And for every measure that God measures out for you, give thanks to God, very, very much.

It's not quite as simple and idealistic and easy as it sounds. On the one hand, there are my grandparents, all murdered in the Holocaust. Then there's my history in the civil rights and anti-war movements, beginning in the early 1960s. And there's also Hannah-Sara's parent's deep commitment to peace and justice, and her own longing for the realization of that dream. On the other hand, every one of our children were good friends with young people who were murdered in terrorist attacks at cafés and schools. Our children have been to more funerals in the last few years than we have been to in our lifetimes. Making an island or garden of peace from the compost of so much loss and suffering from all sides of the conflict is difficult. It requires a lot of weeding and clearing out of so many stones turned up in the fresh soil. It requires a lot of giving and letting go. It is a process that will take years.

In the meantime, our back yard is a little Garden of Eden, a little Paradise. Our garden is a garden of peace and bears the fruits of a small, successful effort at coexistence. Praise be to God. Praise be to Hannah-Sara and her determination to sink her roots here after all her wanderings and challenges. Praise be to the dreams and visions of her mother. Praise be to my parent's dreams, and the routes that brought me from California and psychology, through India and meditation, to Israel and soulful and joyous Jewish contentment. Praise be to our children's courage to keep on going and growing and believing. They are the greatest fruits of our labors.

And for every measure and measure that God measures out for you, give thanks to Him very, very much.

Thank You, God. Thank You very, very much.

NOTES

1. Max Zeller, *The Dream: The Vision of the Night* (Los Angeles: Analytical Psychology Club of Los Angeles, 1975), 2.

2. Abraham Maslow, *Motivation and Personality*, rev. ed. (New York: Harper & Row, 1970), 164.

3. Alan Watts, *The Book: On the Taboo Against Knowing Who You Are* (New York: Pantheon Books, 1966), 8.

4. Menachem Ekstein, *Visions of a Compassionate World: Guided Imagery for Spiritual Growth and Social Transformation*, trans. Yehoshua Starrett (Brooklyn, NY: Lambda Publications, 2001), 28–29.

5. Carlos Castaneda, *A Separate Reality, Further Conversations with Don Juan* (New York: Simon and Schuster, 1971), 186–7.

6. Mordechai Theon, *A Way of Meditation: In the Light of the Kabbalah,* trans. Arieh Rottenberg (Jerusalem: Argaman, 1983).

7. Nachman of Breslov, *Rabbi Nachman's Stories,* trans. Aryeh Kaplan (Jerusalem: Breslov Research Institute, 1983), 34.

ACKNOWLEDGMENTS

A few years ago, Rick Stone offered to do some goals clarification work with me. One exercise, he explained, focused on what I wanted to be doing five years from now. I replied immediately that I wanted to be singing and writing. Since working with him, I went from black-and-white cassettes to full-color CDs, and this book was born. Rick and Elizabeth, thank you both for all the ways you've given support, but most of all, for making me feel so at home in your home, and even more so, in mine.

To everyone who has shown their faith in my writing, singing, teaching, and workshopping: Avraham and Beth Ber, Debra Chwast and her father Milton Mordechai Newmark *z"l* (who recently passed away), Nachman and Miriam Futterman, Arthur and Anya Gordon, David and Betsy Heller, Marty and Chavi Lee, Jeffrey Shalom Mann, Jeffrey and Shira Reiss, Mickey Singer, Jerry and Leah Strauss, Vincent Worms, and Lore Zeller.

I also want to single out my mother-in-law, Beulah Warshall Cohn, who was a teacher and guide at the Brooklyn Botanical Gardens for forty years. She inspires and waters our garden of peace through her life-long devotion to peaceful co-existence, the dignity of humankind, and to honoring the earth and all its beauty.

I can never acknowledge enough what it means to grow up in a family that is so connected to one another throughout our lives no matter our difference or distance. It is such a privilege that my best friends are my brother Dan and my sister Jacqueline. And thank God that tradition continues with their spouses, Nancy and David and their children and grandchildren. Much credit for that goes to our mother, Lore. And to the next generations—my children, their spouses, and my grandchildren: Meera and Shlomo; Manya and David and Mizmor and Elya (who call me *Saba Ruach*, "Grandfather Spirit"); Mordechai; Esther and Sha'arya—thank you for continuing that family love and spirit.

Needless to say, this book would not exist without those whom I have written about. Thank you and please forgive me for any and all misrepresentations or misquotes; all error is due to my faulty memory. And there are so many dear friends and teachers whom I have known and loved—and by whom I have been known and loved and influenced, but have not written about. I have learned so much from you. Thank you and please forgive me for the misrepresentation in your omission. At least there are no misquotes. Thank you all for the stories told, the stories forgotten, and the stories better left untold.

For years I came to Stuart M. Matlins, publisher of Jewish Lights, with manuscripts of my friends, but he kept saying, "David, I'm waiting for *your* manuscript." Thank you, Stuart, for your patience and your faith. If my voice and message are heard in these stories, much credit goes to my primary editor, Arthur Magida, and to Emily Wichland and Mark Ogilbee. If my humor and puns are heard in these stories, all blame goes to me for not listening to their pleas to take them out. My manager, Stuart Schnee, made me take my laptop to write wherever I went. And my dear friends David and Shoshana Cooper gave a lot of start-up time in heart consultations about balancing my writing, teaching, and marriage.

Friends and family know how short, limited, and faulty my memory is. All stories are according to that faulty memory of mine; there is no claim that any of this really happened. The few times I tried to confirm dates or facts with others, their recollections were quite different from mine!

It has been a true blessing and a privilege to have had the experiences and the teachers God has so graciously sent my way. Their only goal was to reveal God's overflowing love and light bursting through everything and everyone in the world. I don't know that I have been able to live up to even a tiny part of the Infinite possibilities of those encounters. I humbly hope and pray that I've done them some justice and that I can still bring a little more of that abundance into the world. I am so grateful and I owe so much.

Hodu L'HaShem Ki Tov. Give thanks to HaShem because it is so good [to give thanks]. I thank God for the gift of my family, friends, teachers, students, and supporters.

NOTES

NOTES

NOTES

NOTES

NOTES

NOTES

NOTES

Theology/Philosophy

Aspects of Rabbinic Theology
By Solomon Schechter. New Introduction by Dr. Neil Gillman.
6 x 9, 448 pp, Quality PB, ISBN 1-879045-24-9 **$19.95**

Broken Tablets: Restoring the Ten Commandments and Ourselves
Edited by Rachel S. Mikva. Introduction by Lawrence Kushner. Afterword by Arnold Jacob Wolf.
6 x 9, 192 pp, Quality PB, ISBN 1-58023-158-6 **$16.95**; Hardcover, ISBN 1-58023-066-0 **$21.9**

Creating an Ethical Jewish Life
A Practical Introduction to Classic Teachings on How to Be a Jew
By Dr. Byron L. Sherwin and Seymour J. Cohen
6 x 9, 336 pp, Quality PB, ISBN 1-58023-114-4 **$19.95**

The Death of Death: Resurrection and Immortality in Jewish Thought
By Dr. Neil Gillman 6 x 9, 336 pp, Quality PB, ISBN 1-58023-081-4 **$18.95**

Evolving Halakhah: A Progressive Approach to Traditional Jewish Law
By Rabbi Dr. Moshe Zemer
6 x 9, 480 pp, Quality PB, ISBN 1-58023-127-6 **$29.95**; Hardcover, ISBN 1-58023-002-4 **$40.0**

Hasidic Tales: Annotated & Explained
By Rabbi Rami Shapiro. Foreword by Andrew Harvey, SkyLight Illuminations series editor.
5½ x 8½, 240 pp, Quality PB, ISBN 1-893361-86-1 **$16.95** *(A SkyLight Paths Book)*

A Heart of Many Rooms: Celebrating the Many Voices within Judaism
By Dr. David Hartman 6 x 9, 352 pp, Quality PB, ISBN 1-58023-156-X **$19.95**

The Hebrew Prophets: Selections Annotated & Explained
Translation & Annotation by Rabbi Rami Shapiro. Foreword by Zalman M. Schachter-Shalomi
5½ x 8½, 224 pp, Quality PB, ISBN 1-59473-037-7 **$16.99** *(A SkyLight Paths book)*

Keeping Faith with the Psalms: Deepen Your Relationship with God Using the
Book of Psalms *By Daniel F. Polish* 6 x 9, 320 pp, Quality PB, ISBN 1-58023-300-7 **$18.99**;
Hardcover, ISBN 1-58023-179-9 **$24.95**

The Last Trial
On the Legends and Lore of the Command to Abraham to Offer Isaac as a Sacrifice
By Shalom Spiegel. New Introduction by Judah Goldin.
6 x 9, 208 pp, Quality PB, ISBN 1-879045-29-X **$18.95**

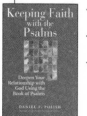

A Living Covenant: The Innovative Spirit in Traditional Judaism
By Dr. David Hartman 6 x 9, 368 pp, Quality PB, ISBN 1-58023-011-3 **$18.95**

Love and Terror in the God Encounter
The Theological Legacy of Rabbi Joseph B. Soloveitchik
By Dr. David Hartman
6 x 9, 240 pp, Quality PB, ISBN 1-58023-176-4 **$19.95**; Hardcover, ISBN 1-58023-112-8 **$25.00**

The Personhood of God: Biblical Theology, Human Faith and the Divine Image
By Dr. Yochanan Muffs; Foreword by Dr. David Hartman
6 x 9, 240 pp, Hardcover, ISBN 1-58023-265-5 **$24.99**

The Spirit of Renewal: Finding Faith after the Holocaust
By Rabbi Edward Feld 6 x 9, 224 pp, Quality PB, ISBN 1-879045-40-0 **$16.95**

Tormented Master: *The Life and Spiritual Quest of Rabbi Nahman of Bratslav*
By Dr. Arthur Green 6 x 9, 416 pp, Quality PB, ISBN 1-879045-11-7 **$19.99**

Your Word Is Fire: The Hasidic Masters on Contemplative Prayer
Edited and translated by Dr. Arthur Green and Barry W. Holtz
6 x 9, 160 pp, Quality PB, ISBN 1-879045-25-7 **$15.95**

I Am Jewish
Personal Reflections Inspired by the Last Words of Daniel Pearl
Almost 150 Jews—both famous and not—from all walks of life, from all around
the world, write about Identity, Heritage, Covenant / Chosenness and Faith,
Humanity and Ethnicity, and *Tikkun Olam* and Justice.
Edited by Judea and Ruth Pearl
6 x 9, 304 pp, Deluxe PB w/flaps, ISBN 1-58023-259-0 **$18.99**; Hardcover, ISBN 1-58023-183-7 **$24.9**
Download a free copy of the *I Am Jewish Teacher's Guide* at our website:
www.jewishlights.com

Spirituality/Women's Interest

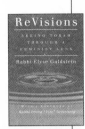

The Quotable Jewish Woman: Wisdom, Inspiration & Humor from
the Mind & Heart *Edited and compiled by Elaine Bernstein Partnow*
The definitive collection of ideas, reflections, humor, and wit of over 300 Jewish women.
6 x 9, 496 pp, Hardcover, ISBN 1-58023-193-4 **$29.99**

Lifecycles, Vol. 1: Jewish Women on Life Passages & Personal Milestones
Edited and with introductions by Rabbi Debra Orenstein 6 x 9, 480 pp, Quality PB, ISBN 1-58023-018-0 **$19.95**

Lifecycles, Vol. 2: Jewish Women on Biblical Themes in Contemporary Life
Edited and with introductions by Rabbi Debra Orenstein and Rabbi Jane Rachel Litman
6 x 9, 464 pp, Quality PB, ISBN 1-58023-019-9 **$19.95**

Moonbeams: A Hadassah Rosh Hodesh Guide *Edited by Carol Diament, Ph.D.*
8½ x 11, 240 pp, Quality PB, ISBN 1-58023-099-7 **$20.00**

ReVisions: Seeing Torah through a Feminist Lens *By Rabbi Elyse Goldstein*
5½ x 8½, 224 pp, Quality PB, ISBN 1-58023-117-9 **$16.95**

White Fire: A Portrait of Women Spiritual Leaders in America
By Rabbi Malka Drucker. Photographs by Gay Block.
7 x 10, 320 pp, 30+ b/w photos, Hardcover, ISBN 1-893361-64-0 **$24.95** *(A SkyLight Paths book)*

Women of the Wall: Claiming Sacred Ground at Judaism's Holy Site
Edited by Phyllis Chesler and Rivka Haut 6 x 9, 496 pp, b/w photos, Hardcover, ISBN 1-58023-161-6 **$34.95**

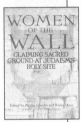

The Women's Haftarah Commentary: New Insights from Women Rabbis on
the 54 Weekly Haftarah Portions, the 5 Megillot & Special Shabbatot
Edited by Rabbi Elyse Goldstein 6 x 9, 560 pp, Hardcover, ISBN 1-58023-133-0 **$39.99**

The Women's Torah Commentary: New Insights from Women Rabbis on the 54
Weekly Torah Portions *Edited by Rabbi Elyse Goldstein*
6 x 9, 496 pp, Hardcover, ISBN 1-58023-076-8 **$34.95**

The Year Mom Got Religion: One Woman's Midlife Journey into Judaism
By Lee Meyerhoff Hendler 6 x 9, 208 pp, Quality PB, ISBN 1-58023-070-9 **$15.95**

See Holidays for *The Women's Passover Companion: Women's Reflections on
the Festival of Freedom* and *The Women's Seder Sourcebook: Rituals &
Readings for Use at the Passover Seder.* Also see Bar/Bat Mitzvah for *The JGirl's
Guide: The Young Jewish Woman's Handbook for Coming of Age.*

Travel

Israel—A Spiritual Travel Guide, 2nd Edition
A Companion for the Modern Jewish Pilgrim
By Rabbi Lawrence A. Hoffman 4¾ x 10, 256 pp, Quality PB, illus., ISBN 1-58023-261-2 **$18.99**
Also Available: **The Israel Mission Leader's Guide** ISBN 1-58023-085-7 **$4.95**

12 Steps

100 Blessings Every Day Daily Twelve Step Recovery Affirmations, Exercises
for Personal Growth & Renewal Reflecting Seasons of the Jewish Year
By Rabbi Kerry M. Olitzky. Foreword by Rabbi Neil Gillman.
One-day-at-a-time monthly format. Reflects on the rhythm of the Jewish calen-
dar to bring insight to recovery from addictions.
4½ x 6½, 432 pp, Quality PB, ISBN 1-879045-30-3 **$15.99**

Recovery from Codependence: A Jewish Twelve Steps Guide to Healing Your Soul
By Rabbi Kerry M. Olitzky 6 x 9, 160 pp, Quality PB, ISBN 1-879045-32-X **$13.95**

Renewed Each Day: Daily Twelve Step Recovery Meditations Based on the Bible
By Rabbi Kerry M. Olitzky and Aaron Z.
Vol. 1—Genesis & Exodus: 6 x 9, 224 pp, Quality PB, ISBN 1-879045-12-5 **$14.95**
Vol. 2—Leviticus, Numbers & Deuteronomy: 6 x 9, 280 pp, Quality PB, ISBN 1-879045-13-3 **$14.95**

Twelve Jewish Steps to Recovery: A Personal Guide to Turning from Alcoholism &
Other Addictions—Drugs, Food, Gambling, Sex...
By Rabbi Kerry M. Olitzky and Stuart A. Copans, M.D. Preface by Abraham J. Twerski, M.D.
6 x 9, 144 pp, Quality PB, ISBN 1-879045-09-5 **$14.95**

Children's Books

What You Will See Inside a Synagogue
By Rabbi Lawrence A. Hoffman and Dr. Ron Wolfson; Full-color photos by Bill Aron

A colorful, fun-to-read introduction that explains the ways and whys of
Jewish worship and religious life. Full-page photos; concise but informative
descriptions of the objects used, the clergy and laypeople who have specific
roles, and much more. For ages 6 & up.

8½ x 10½, 32 pp, Full-color photos, Hardcover, ISBN 1-59473-012-1 **$17.99** *(A SkyLight Paths book)*

Because Nothing Looks Like God
By Lawrence and Karen Kushner

What is God like? Introduces children to the possibilities of spiritual life. Real-life
examples of happiness and sadness invite us to explore, together with our children, the questions we all have about God.

11 x 8½, 32 pp, Full-color illus., Hardcover, ISBN 1-58023-092-X **$16.95** *For ages 4 & up*

Also Available: **Because Nothing Looks Like God Teacher's Guide**
8½ x 11, 22 pp, PB, ISBN 1-58023-140-3 **$6.95** *For ages 5–8*

  Board Book Companions to *Because Nothing Looks Like God*
5 x 5, 24 pp, Full-color illus., SkyLight Paths Board Books *For ages 0–4*

What Does God Look Like? ISBN 1-893361-23-3 **$7.95**

How Does God Make Things Happen? ISBN 1-893361-24-1 **$7.95**

Where Is God? ISBN 1-893361-17-9 **$7.99**

The 11th Commandment: Wisdom from Our Children
By The Children of America

"If there were an Eleventh Commandment, what would it be?" Children of many
religious denominations across America answer in their own drawings and words.
8 x 10, 48 pp, Full-color illus., Hardcover, ISBN 1-879045-46-X **$16.95** *For all ages*

Jerusalem of Gold: Jewish Stories of the Enchanted City
Retold by Howard Schwartz. Full-color illus. by Neil Waldman.

A beautiful and engaging collection of historical and legendary stories for children. Based on Talmud, midrash, Jewish folklore, and mystical and Hasidic sources.
8 x 10, 64 pp, Full-color illus., Hardcover, ISBN 1-58023-149-7 **$18.95** *For ages 7 & up*

The Book of Miracles: A Young Person's Guide to Jewish Spiritual Awareness
By Lawrence Kushner. All-new illustrations by the author.
6 x 9, 96 pp, 2-color illus., Hardcover, ISBN 1-879045-78-8 **$16.95** *For ages 9–13*

In Our Image: God's First Creatures
By Nancy Sohn Swartz
9 x 12, 32 pp, Full-color illus., Hardcover, ISBN 1-879045-99-0 **$16.95** *For ages 4 & up*

Also Available as a Board Book: **How Did the Animals Help God?**
5 x 5, 24 pp, Board, Full-color illus., ISBN 1-59473-044-X **$7.99** *For ages 0–4 (A SkyLight Paths book)*

From SKYLIGHT PATHS PUBLISHING

Becoming Me: A Story of Creation
By Martin Boroson. Full-color illus. by Christopher Gilvan-Cartwright.

Told in the personal "voice" of the Creator, a story about creation and relationship that is about each one of us.
8 x 10, 32 pp, Full-color illus., Hardcover, ISBN 1-893361-11-X **$16.95** *For ages 4 & up*

Ten Amazing People: And How They Changed the World
By Maura D. Shaw. Foreword by Dr. Robert Coles. Full-color illus. by Stephen Marchesi.

Black Elk • Dorothy Day • Malcolm X • Mahatma Gandhi • Martin Luther King,
Jr. • Mother Teresa • Janusz Korczak • Desmond Tutu • Thich Nhat Hanh •
Albert Schweitzer.

8½ x 11, 48 pp, Full-color illus., Hardcover, ISBN 1-893361-47-0 **$17.95** *For ages 7 & up*

Where Does God Live? *By August Gold and Matthew J. Perlman*

Helps young readers develop a personal understanding of God.
10 x 8½, 32 pp, Full-color photo illus., Quality PB, ISBN 1-893361-39-X **$8.99** *For ages 3–6*

Children's Books
by Sandy Eisenberg Sasso

Adam & Eve's First Sunset: God's New Day
Engaging new story explores fear and hope, faith and gratitude in ways that will delight kids and adults—inspiring us to bless each of God's days and nights.
9 x 12, 32 pp, Full-color illus., Hardcover, ISBN 1-58023-177-2 **$17.95** *For ages 4 & up*

But God Remembered
Stories of Women from Creation to the Promised Land
Four different stories of women—Lillith, Serach, Bityah, and the Daughters of Z—teach us important values through their faith and actions.
9 x 12, 32 pp, Full-color illus., Hardcover, ISBN 1-879045-43-5 **$16.95** *For ages 8 & up*

Cain & Abel: Finding the Fruits of Peace
Shows children that we have the power to deal with anger in positive ways. Provides questions for kids and adults to explore together.
9 x 12, 32 pp, Full-color illus., Hardcover, ISBN 1-58023-123-3 **$16.95** *For ages 5 & up*

God in Between
If you wanted to find God, where would you look? This magical, mythical tale teaches that God can be found where we are: within all of us and the relationships between us.
9 x 12, 32 pp, Full-color illus., Hardcover, ISBN 1-879045-86-9 **$16.95** *For ages 4 & up*

God's Paintbrush: Special 10th Anniversary Edition
Wonderfully interactive, invites children of all faiths and backgrounds to encounter God through moments in their own lives. Provides questions adult and child can explore together.
11 x 8½, 32 pp, Full-color illus., Hardcover, ISBN 1-58023-195-0 **$17.95** *For ages 4 & up*

Also Available: **God's Paintbrush Teacher's Guide**
8½ x 11, 32 pp, PB, ISBN 1-879045-57-5 **$8.95**

God's Paintbrush Celebration Kit
A Spiritual Activity Kit for Teachers and Students of All Faiths, All Backgrounds
Additional activity sheets available:
8-Student Activity Sheet Pack (40 sheets/5 sessions), ISBN 1-58023-058-X **$19.95**
Single-Student Activity Sheet Pack (5 sessions), ISBN 1-58023-059-8 **$3.95**

In God's Name
Like an ancient myth in its poetic text and vibrant illustrations, this award-winning modern fable about the search for God's name celebrates the diversity and, at the same time, the unity of all people.
9 x 12, 32 pp, Full-color illus., Hardcover, ISBN 1-879045-26-5 **$16.99** *For ages 4 & up*

Also Available as a Board Book: **What Is God's Name?**
5 x 5, 24 pp, Board, Full-color illus., ISBN 1-893361-10-1 **$7.99** *For ages 0–4* *(A SkyLight Paths book)*

Also Available: **In God's Name video and study guide**
Computer animation, original music, and children's voices. 18 min. **$29.99**

Also Available in Spanish: **El nombre de Dios**
9 x 12, 32 pp, Full-color illus., Hardcover, ISBN 1-893361-63-2 **$16.95** *(A SkyLight Paths book)*

Noah's Wife: The Story of Naamah
When God tells Noah to bring the animals of the world onto the ark, God also calls on Naamah, Noah's wife, to save each plant on Earth. Based on an ancient text.
9 x 12, 32 pp, Full-color illus., Hardcover, ISBN 1-58023-134-9 **$16.95** *For ages 4 & up*

Also Available as a Board Book: **Naamah, Noah's Wife**
5 x 5, 24 pp, Full-color illus., Board, ISBN 1-893361-56-X **$7.95** *For ages 0–4* *(A SkyLight Paths book)*

For Heaven's Sake: Finding God in Unexpected Places
9 x 12, 32 pp, Full-color illus., Hardcover, ISBN 1-58023-054-7 **$16.95** *For ages 4 & up*

God Said Amen: Finding the Answers to Our Prayers
9 x 12, 32 pp, Full-color illus., Hardcover, ISBN 1-58023-080-6 **$16.95** *For ages 4 & up*

Current Events/History

The Story of the Jews: A 4,000-Year Adventure—A Graphic History Boo
Written & illustrated by Stan Mack
Witty, illustrated narrative of all the major happenings from biblical times to th
twenty-first century. 6 x 9, 288 pp, illus., Quality PB, ISBN 1-58023-155-1 **$16.95**

Hannah Senesh: Her Life and Diary, the First Complete Edition
By Hannah Senesh; Foreword by Marge Piercy; Preface by Eitan Senesh
6 x 9, 352 pp, Hardcover, ISBN 1-58023-212-4 **$24.99**

The Jewish Prophet: Visionary Words from Moses and Miriam to Henrietta Szold
and A. J. Heschel *By Rabbi Michael J. Shire*
6½ x 8½, 128 pp, 123 full-color illus., Hardcover, ISBN 1-58023-168-3 **Special gift price $14.95**

Shared Dreams: Martin Luther King, Jr. & the Jewish Community
By Rabbi Marc Schneier. Preface by Martin Luther King III.
6 x 9, 240 pp, Hardcover, ISBN 1-58023-062-8 **$24.95**

"Who Is a Jew?": Conversations, Not Conclusions *By Meryl Hyman*
6 x 9, 272 pp, Quality PB, ISBN 1-58023-052-0 **$16.95**

Ecology

Ecology & the Jewish Spirit: Where Nature & the Sacred Meet
Edited by Ellen Bernstein 6 x 9, 288 pp, Quality PB, ISBN 1-58023-082-2 **$16.95**

Torah of the Earth: Exploring 4,000 Years of Ecology in Jewish Thought
Vol. 1: Biblical Israel: One Land, One People; Rabbinic Judaism: One People, Many Lands
Vol. 2: Zionism: One Land, Two Peoples; Eco-Judaism: One Earth, Many Peoples
Edited by Rabbi Arthur Waskow
Vol. 1: 6 x 9, 272 pp, Quality PB, ISBN 1-58023-086-5 **$19.95**
Vol. 2: 6 x 9, 336 pp, Quality PB, ISBN 1-58023-087-3 **$19.95**

The Way Into Judaism and the Environment
By Jeremy Benstein, PhD
6 x 9, 225 pp (est.), Hardcover, ISBN 1-58023-268-X **$24.99**

Grief/Healing

Against the Dying of the Light: A Parent's Story of Love, Loss and Hope
By Leonard Fein
5½ x 8½, 176 pp, Quality PB, ISBN 1-58023-197-7 **$15.99;** Hardcover, ISBN 1-58023-110-1 **$19.95**

Grief in Our Seasons: A Mourner's Kaddish Companion *By Rabbi Kerry M. Olitzky*
4½ x 6½, 448 pp, Quality PB, ISBN 1-879045-55-9 **$15.95**

Healing of Soul, Healing of Body: Spiritual Leaders Unfold the Strength & Solace
in Psalms *Edited by Rabbi Simkha Y. Weintraub, C.S.W.*
6 x 9, 128 pp, 2-color illus. text, Quality PB, ISBN 1-879045-31-1 **$14.99**

Jewish Paths toward Healing and Wholeness: A Personal Guide to Dealing with
Suffering *By Rabbi Kerry M. Olitzky. Foreword by Debbie Friedman.*
6 x 9, 192 pp, Quality PB, ISBN 1-58023-068-7 **$15.95**

Mourning & Mitzvah, 2nd Edition: A Guided Journal for Walking the Mourner's
Path through Grief to Healing *By Anne Brener, L.C.S.W.*
7½ x 9, 304 pp, Quality PB, ISBN 1-58023-113-6 **$19.95**

The Perfect Stranger's Guide to Funerals and Grieving Practices
A Guide to Etiquette in Other People's Religious Ceremonies *Edited by Stuart M. Matlins*
6 x 9, 240 pp, Quality PB, ISBN 1-893361-20-9 **$16.95** *(A SkyLight Paths book)*

Tears of Sorrow, Seeds of Hope: A Jewish Spiritual Companion for Infertility and
Pregnancy Loss *By Rabbi Nina Beth Cardin*
6 x 9, 192 pp, Quality PB, ISBN 1-58023-017-2 **$19.95**

A Time to Mourn, A Time to Comfort, 2nd Edition: A Guide to Jewish
Bereavement and Comfort *By Dr. Ron Wolfson*
7 x 9, 336 pp, Quality PB, ISBN 1-58023-253-1 **$19.99**

When a Grandparent Dies: A Kid's Own Remembering Workbook for Dealing
with Shiva and the Year Beyond *By Nechama Liss-Levinson, Ph.D.*
8 x 10, 48 pp, 2-color text, Hardcover, ISBN 1-879045-44-3 **$15.95** *For ages 7–13*